CAMBRIDGE MUSIC HANDBOOKS

Mozart: The 'Jupiter' Symphony

CAMBRIDGE MUSIC HANDBOOKS

GENERAL EDITOR Julian Rushton

Cambridge Music Handbooks provide accessible introductions to major musical works, written by the most informed commentators in the field.

With the concert-goer, performer and student in mind, the books present essential information on the historical and musical context, the composition, and the performance and reception history of each work, or group of works, as well as critical discussion of the music.

Other published titles

Bach: The Brandenburg Concertos MALCOLM BOYD
Bach: Mass in B Minor JOHN BUTT
Beethoven: *Missa solemnis* WILLIAM DRABKIN
Beethoven: Symphony No. 9 NICHOLAS COOK
Berg: Violin Concerto ANTHONY POPLE
Chopin: The Four Ballades JIM SAMSON
Handel: *Messiah* DONALD BURROWS
Haydn: *The Creation* NICHOLAS TEMPERLEY
Haydn: String Quartets, Op. 50 W. DEAN SUTCLIFFE
Janáček: *Glagolitic Mass* PAUL WINGFIELD
Mahler: Symphony No. 3 PETER FRANKLIN
Mendelssohn: *The Hebrides* and other overtures R. LARRY TODD
Musorgsky: *Pictures at an Exhibition* MICHAEL RUSS
Schoenberg: *Pierrot lunaire* JONATHAN DUNSBY
Schubert: *Die schöne Müllerin* SUSAN YOUENS
Schumann: Fantasie, Op. 17 NICHOLAS MARSTON
Sibelius: Symphony No. 5 JAMES HEPOKOSKI
Strauss: *Also sprach Zarathustra* JOHN WILLIAMSON
Stravinsky: *Oedipus rex* STEPHEN WALSH

Mozart: The 'Jupiter' Symphony

No. 41 in C major, K. 551

Elaine R. Sisman

Associate Professor of Music,
Columbia University

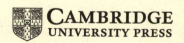

CAMBRIDGE
UNIVERSITY PRESS

Published by the Press Syndicate of the University of Cambridge
The Pitt Building, Trumpington Street, Cambridge CB2 1RP
40 West 20th Street, New York, NY 10011–4211, USA
10 Stamford Road, Oakleigh, Victoria 3166, Australia

First published 1993

Printed in Great Britain at the University Press, Cambridge

A catalogue record for this book is available from the British Library

Library of Congress cataloguing in publication data
Sisman, Elaine Rochelle.
Mozart: The 'Jupiter' symphony / Elaine Sisman.
p. cm. – (Cambridge music handbooks)
Includes bibliographical references and index.
ISBN 0 521 40069 4 (hardback) – ISBN 0 521 40924 1 (paperback)
1. Mozart, Wolfgang Amadeus, 1756–1791. Symphonies, K. 551, C major
I. Title. II. Series.
ML410.M9S56 1993
784.2'184–dc20 92–39074 CIP MN

ISBN 0 521 40069 4 hardback
ISBN 0 521 40924 1 paperback

AH

2693 2362

For my mother and father

Contents

Contents

Tables

Preface

Had Johann Peter Salomon not commissioned Haydn to write twelve symphonies for his concert series in London, he still would have earned his berth in music history by bestowing upon Mozart's last symphony, so the story goes, the nickname "Jupiter." Vincent Novello described a conversation with Franz Xaver Mozart: "Mozart's son said he considered the Finale to his father's sinfonie in C – which Salomon christened the Jupiter – to be the highest triumph of instrumental composition, and I agree with him."[1] Indeed, the extraordinary finale, with its density of musical utterance, recalls Mozart's own remark to his father Leopold that the third act of *Idomeneo* was nearly finished, and that it "will turn out to be *at least* as good as the first two – in fact, I believe, infinitely better – and I think that it may be said with truth, *finis coronat opus*."[2] That the end crowns the work is surely one of the most historically significant features of his "Jupiter" Symphony, which looks forward to such "teleological" works as Beethoven's Fifth and Ninth Symphonies. But the mere fact of a weighty conclusion has been less important in the reception of the work than the high seriousness of fugal technique impinging upon a sonata design, especially the dazzling display of double fugue and canon in the coda. Mozart's last symphony has not lacked for interpreters, as the numerous entries in bibliographies published in the *Mozart-Jahrbuch* and in Neal Zaslaw's recent book on the Mozart symphonies make clear; yet there are no monographs in English.[3]

The organization of this book appears at first glance to chart a course from the general to the specific: from the genre of symphony in Mozart's time and its principal aesthetic characteristics to Mozart's own compositional history in the summer of 1788, to a study of each of the four individual movements of the "Jupiter." But the four movement-studies are to an extent based on broad areas of inquiry, some of them of fairly recent vintage in musicological criticism, analysis, and scholarship of the later eighteenth century. I hope to make as vivid a case as possible for the connection of musical detail to larger issues.

At times, the other two celebrated symphonies of the summer of 1788 will be summoned for comparison. Indeed, in light of the canonical number three, creating the trilogies, trinities, and triumvirates sanctioned by history, religion, and popular culture, the last three symphonies of Mozart are so overdetermined as an inevitable grouping, not to mention as the locus of supreme value in his instrumental music, that a consideration of but one of them seems to call for constant contextualization. But even the three symphonies require the additional context of other Viennese works, such as the "Prague" Symphony and the piano concertos of 1784–6, for a full accounting.[4] Nonetheless, I hope to keep the spotlight as much on the "Jupiter" as possible.

I am grateful to Columbia University for granting me the sabbatical leave that enabled me to complete this book. I would also like to thank Penny Souster and Julian Rushton for their encouragement of this project; Stanley Sadie for inviting me to the Royal Musical Association Mozart Conference in August 1991, where a number of the ideas in this book received their first public hearing; and those colleagues who offered trenchant comments in response to those ideas: James Webster, Leo Treitler, Michael Long, Christoph Wolff, Laurence Dreyfus, Karol Berger, Mitchell Morris, and other members of the audiences to whom I spoke about issues surrounding the "Jupiter" Symphony, at Princeton University, University of California at Berkeley, Stanford University, State University of New York at Buffalo, and the City University of New York Graduate Center. An invitation from Westfield Center for Early Keyboard Studies to present papers at its symposium on "Mozart's Nature, Mozart's World" at the Boston Museum of Fine Arts in 1991 enabled me to develop my ideas on the sublime; I am grateful to Lynn Edwards, director of the Center, for her support. Finally, my husband Marty Fridson deserves special thanks for his willingness to be a sounding board at any hour, as do Arielle and Daniel for their diversionary tactics. This book is dedicated to my parents, Irving and Margot Sisman, who gave me a childhood filled with music.

The symphony in Mozart's Vienna

Symphonies were ubiquitous in musical life of the late eighteenth century. In Vienna, virtually every public concert began with a symphony, and the evidence suggests they concluded with one, or with a symphony finale, as well. Moreover, every possible performing venue featured symphonies, and writers often drew distinctions among three kinds of symphonies based on these venues and the styles common to each: concert or chamber symphonies, performed in concert rooms, including theaters temporarily devoted to concerts (such as the Vienna Burgtheater during Lent), the larger salons of the nobility, and casinos and gardens; theater symphonies, including opera overtures and music performed before and between the acts of plays; and church symphonies, comprising overtures to oratorios and sacred cantatas as well as symphonies played during the liturgy.[1] By the end of the first quarter of the nineteenth century, the genre "symphony" needed no qualification: it was simply a multi-movement piece for orchestra, a symphony in the modern sense.

The "overture" function of a concert symphony, with subsequent portions given to vocal and instrumental soloists performing arias, concertos, and improvisations, is clarified by this often-cited program of Mozart's concert in the Burgtheater on 23 March 1783, at which Emperor Joseph II and perhaps Gluck were present:[2]

"Haffner" Symphony, K. 385, I–III (?)[3]
Aria (No. 11) from *Idomeneo*, K. 366
Piano Concerto in C major, K. 415/387b
Recitative and Aria for soprano, K. 369
Symphonie concertante, III and IV of Serenade, K. 320
Piano Concerto in D major, K. 175 with new finale, K. 382
Aria (No. 16) from *Lucio Silla*, K. 135
Short fugue for piano, improvised
Variations for piano, K. 398/416e
Variations for piano, K. 455
Recitative and Rondo for soprano, K. 416
"Haffner" Symphony, IV

Symphonies not infrequently began with the broad gestures and loud dynamics of a call to order, something that László Somfai has called a 'noise-killer' effect.[4] But this functional quality to symphonies should not obscure the fact that they were admired and respectfully reviewed, often helping to establish and enhance a composer's reputation. Neal Zaslaw stresses that symphonies in Mozart's time were considered occasional, strictly functional music, composed on an *ad hoc* basis for *ad hoc* personnel.[5] Yet by the 1780s and 1790s, they were considered the touchstone of instrumental style: writers of composition manuals routinely saw the symphony as normative, in multi-movement format and in style, and designed their compositional instruction on it. The most famous of these writers is probably Heinrich Christoph Koch, who described every other instrumental genre in relation to typical symphonic procedures.[6] Distilling these writings suggests that the style embodied by symphonies stood in contrast to a "sonata style," each characterized by a particular kind of expression deriving from a melodic style of large gestures and overlapping cadences in the former and "elaboration, nuance, and detail" in the latter.[7] Michael Broyles argues that, according to these criteria at least, the symphony style became more prevalent in the 1790s, affecting chamber and piano music; future studies will need to address this point. Just as concert halls and pianos increased in size at this time, chamber music and piano music began to be played in public, and thus required a breadth of scale different from music for, as Koch described sets of variations, *Privatvergnügen*.[8]

The overlap between Mozart's decade in Vienna (1781–91) and the decade of Joseph II's sole rule (1780–90; he reigned together with his mother Maria Theresia after his father's death in 1765) has made plausible the assertion that Mozart's search for freedom from the constraints of his employment in Salzburg and independence from his father and the hated Archbishop resonated with the reformist zeal of the enlightened monarch. Andrew Steptoe goes so far as to adduce as reasons for Mozart's continued residence in Vienna during the lean late 1780s both the strength of Mozart's sympathy for the Emperor and the tolerant, respectful climate the Emperor had created in Vienna.[9] Certainly Joseph's opening to the people of Vienna many areas previously reserved to the privileged classes, including the Prater and the Augarten (in which concerts were subsequently held), broadened the possible venues for musical culture to flourish. It is possible to see the brilliant expansion of public concerts in the 1780s as part of this new focus on enjoyments for the people – the inscription over the Augarten gate read "These pleasure grounds are dedicated to all men, by their protector."[10] But patrons among the nobility remained essential for a successful career.

Symphonies for patrons and the public

Because Joseph II eschewed the pomp and lavish court occasions of earlier monarchs, members of the nobility – "twenty princes and sixty counts with their numerous relatives" – took up the slack in sponsoring high-society events, including concerts.[11] The private salons of many of these aristocrats helped fill Mozart's calendar during one extraordinary five-and-a-half week period covering March 1784, when he played twenty-two concerts in thirty-eight days: every Thursday at Prince Galitzin's, every Monday and Friday at Count Johann Esterházy's, three Saturdays at the pianist Richter's series of subscription concerts in Trattner's house (Trattnerhof), in addition to his own series of three private subscription concerts on Wednesdays in the same place, and two public concerts in the theater. Mozart stated that the same people who invited him to no fewer than fourteen salons then paid to hear him six times by subscription; he boasted that he had over one hundred subscribers and "shall easily get another thirty."[12] He also noted, poignantly, that he had little time to compose since he taught every morning and played every evening.

Possibly the preponderance of private venues for his concerts in this period made it unnecessary for him to write symphonies, because only the wealthier patrons had their own orchestras. But even the previous year he had seen no necessity to compose a new symphony for the March 1783 concert (program given above), asking his father instead to send several much earlier symphonies out of which he earmarked the "Haffner" for the public.[13] Given the enormous popularity of the new Finale he composed in 1782 to his Salzburg concerto, K. 175 (known as the Rondo in D major, K. 382, even though it is a set of variations), he may have considered revising movements here and there in older works in hopes of scoring a similar – easily won – success. In private concerts, string quartets were sometimes played instead of symphonies, and of course keyboard works were more prominent.[14] Mozart's special talents on the keyboard commanded more attention in the mid-1780s, and for concertos, a quartet of strings and a few winds may have been considered a group of sufficient size. After all, his first set of subscription concertos, K. 413–15, had been specially designed, he claimed, for performance with string quartet and winds *ad libitum*, and the E♭-major concerto for Barbara Ployer, K. 449, exploited a chamber-music style of contrapuntal and varied textures. Several of the self-described "*große Konzerte*," on the other hand, were written expressly for the public concerts in the theater.[15]

Although Vienna had virtually no regular public concert series, there appears to have been a veritable frenzy of performing activity during Lent and Advent, when plays and operas could not be performed in the Burgtheater and Kärntnertortheater. Four or five of these concerts were given by the Tonkünstler-Sozietät (usually two in each season), begun by Gassmann in 1772 for the benefit of widows and orphans. Boasting a very large orchestra in which most professional musicians were proud to perform, the Society was best known for its performances of oratorios, during which instrumental pieces like concertos were performed as entr'actes, as well as more diverse evening-length concerts, such as the *grosse musikalische Akademie* of 17 March 1777 at which a symphony by Ordonez was played.[16] Mary Sue Morrow classifies the remaining types of public concerts in Vienna, between the mid-1770s and about 1810, in four groups: Virtuoso Benefits, in which Mozart's concerts "for his own benefit" would clearly fall; Charity Fundraisers, taking their cue from the Tonkünstler-Sozietät in the 1790s; Entrepreneur Subscription Series, though these appear to center around only Philipp Jacques Martin (who in moving from the Mehlgrube in 1781 to the Augarten in 1782 enlisted Mozart for his morning concerts) and Ignaz Schuppanzigh in the late 1790s; and finally a few series organized by various Friends of Music Societies, such as the summer concerts in the Belvedere Palace gardens between 1785 and 1787.[17] Composers would typically seek more than one of these venues for maximum exposure. For example, after Dittersdorf wrote twelve symphonies on Ovid's *Metamorphoses* in 1785, he sought to have them performed in Vienna, deciding on six in the Augarten and six in the theater (the latter at least in part because the weather was bad).[18]

Haydn's career during the 1780s has several features in common with Mozart, even though in external circumstance Haydn remained a regular *Kapellmeister* to the Esterházy family, one of the wealthiest in Hapsburg lands. At virtually the same time that Mozart returned in defeat to Salzburg after his Parisian debacle, and started to plot his next attempt at breaking free – January 1779 – Haydn renegotiated his contract with Prince Nikolaus Esterházy in order to take advantage of his ever-increasing fame. From being a wholly-owned subsidiary of the Prince, Haydn himself now owned the rights to his works and was able to negotiate directly with publishers and outside concert organizations on a large, international scale. Indeed, after 1785 Haydn wrote no more symphonies for Eszterháza, instead preparing them for the Concerts de la Loge Olympique (Nos. 82–7) and the Comte d'Ogny (Nos. 90–2) in Paris, for the violinist-businessman Johann Tost (Nos. 88–9), and for Johann Peter Salomon in London (Nos. 93–104). An earlier set of three, Nos. 76–8 of 1783, were written for a planned London trip that never materialized. The international scope of the second half of Haydn's career thus stemmed from a position of greater independence from his patron, precisely the kind of position that Mozart was unable to win for himself while still employed by the Archbishop.

The price of Haydn's success was being forced to adjust to the new realities of composing for an unknown audience and orchestra. For almost two decades Haydn had trained his ensemble and written for it at Eisenstadt and Eszterháza. He knew the skills of his performers, the size and acoustics of his concert rooms, and an audience whose taste he could form gradually.[19] The 1780s opened the world to him, and he composed for that creation of the late eighteenth century, a musical public. Mozart, whose career had unfolded on an international scale from his childhood, expressed no qualms about the anonymous audience.

Haydn's "Paris" Symphonies were commissioned by a Masonic lodge which held concerts.[20] The Masonic lodges in Vienna had large-scale vocal music; did they also have large-scale orchestral music? The available evidence suggests little beyond the presence of ceremonial music, but with certain interesting exceptions. Outside the so-called "Masonic Funeral Music," K. 477, everything Mozart wrote for his lodge included voices, even one of the versions of K. 477, but certainly groups of instrumentalists were marshalled for such performances.[21] In addition to meetings at which his Masonic works were performed, Mozart participated in three lodge concerts: 20 October 1785 at Anton Stadler's lodge for the benefit of two basset-horn players, where Mozart improvised; 15 December 1785 at "Zur gekrönten Hoffnung" for the benefit of David and Springer, where he played a piano concerto and improvised; and 12 January 1788 at an academy of "Zur gekrönten Hoffnung" in honor of the wedding of Archduke Francis and Princess Elisabeth Wilhelmine of Württemberg.[22] The program at the second of these included two symphonies by Wranitzky, the leader of Johann Esterházy's musical establishment, "specially composed" for the lodge.[23] It is possible that further research will turn up other such events.

Symphonies on concert programs

For every attentive listener like Burney, who thrilled to the symphonies performed before and between the acts of plays and at the beginnings of concerts, there was a multitude of audience members who were rude or oblivious during the symphonies, as reported by Nicolai in 1781 and by various correspondents of the *Allgemeine musikalische Zeitung*.[24] Haydn even sought to have his works put in the second half of the Salomon concerts in

London, according to his biographer Dies, because

> The first half was usually disturbed in all sorts of ways by the noise of latecomers. Not a few people came from well set tables (where the men, after the custom of their country, stayed sitting and drinking after the women had proceeded at the end of the meal into another room), took a comfortable place in the concert hall, and there were so overpowered by the magic of music that a deep sleep overcame them. Now imagine whether in a concert hall where not a few but many persons with their snuffling or snoring or hanging of heads present the true listeners with something to chatter about or more probably to laugh at, whether quiet can reign there?[25]

Actually, after the first few concerts in each London season, quite a number began with a Haydn symphony, so he was not entirely successful in avoiding the initial distractions.[26]

It seems important to ask, then, what purpose the symphony served in its ungrateful spot as overture. Morrow points out that it seems anachronistic to criticize the role of "noise-killer" for the symphony when there were few other ways to attract attention to the beginning of the concert: candles could not be dimmed, after all, and the conductor, being part of the ensemble, did not make a separate dramatic entrance.[27] With respect to actual overtures to operas and plays, music theorists were quite specific about the role of that introductory music, usually suggesting ways to prepare the listener generally for the affects of the evening's drama.[28] But Abbé Vogler suggestively remarked that a theater symphony ought to "stir the spectator and prepare him by lowering his resistance to the force of those passions that will be represented on the stage. Displaying fire and splendor, it must enthrall the listener by virtue of the force of its harmonious organization."[29] Would a concert-goer need to have his or her resistance lowered to an evening of concertos and arias? Or rather, does the array of affects in a typical symphony, from the "fire and splendor" of the first movement through the Andante's idyll, the graceful and direct dance movement, to the quick and tuneful finale, prepare the listener by traversing some of the possibilities of contemporary musical style? In mixing single-movement and multi-movement, vocal and instrumental works, the concert-planner clearly strove for a pleasant variety; symphonies and symphony movements were sometimes dispersed throughout a program. We also need to take into account the "framing" aspect of a symphony at the beginning and end of a program, made especially cogent if the finale of the opening symphony is played or even repeated (as in Mozart's concert of March 1783).[30] Today's concert programs are often "thematic" or genre-specific; perhaps the coherence of experience provided by a frame was the late-eighteenth-century equivalent. In those concerts that moved from the orchestral to the soloistic and back to the orchestral, the programs metaphorically traversed a rhetorical pattern: from "general" introduction to "specific" arguments to "general" summing-up. (Chapter 2 will argue for the importance of rhetoric in musical thought of this period.)

In addition, the symphony was the only piece on a mixed program that enabled the audience to concentrate on the skill of the composer without distraction by the need to evaluate the technical proficiency of soloists. The earlier vogue for symphonies featuring *concertante* instruments in the 1760s and early 1770s, as wealthier courts sought to show off the professional caliber of their musicians, had largely passed; by the 1780s, *concertante* instruments were more likely to be given prominent roles in particular thematic areas of the piece (especially the second group and development), individual variations, trios of minuets, or in the occasional "wind cadenza," as in the slow movements of two of Haydn's "Paris" Symphonies, Nos. 84 and 87.[31] That over one quarter of the symphonies performed in Vienna during the 1780s were by Haydn suggests not only his popularity but also that the quality of opening symphonies was a concern of the organizers.[32] But despite the variable styles of opening and closing movements especially, whether by Haydn or Mozart themselves, or by the other composers actually named on programs of the 1780s (J. C. Bach, Dittersdorf, Eybler, Fischer, Gluck, Huber, Kozeluch, Pleyel, Riegl, van Swieten, Winter, Wranitzky),[33] the vast majority of symphonies began with a tutti *forte* gesture; the audience may not necessarily have expected any particular *kind* of "noise-killer," "intrada"-style opening, nor a romping rondo finale, but expectations existed nonetheless.

Public expectations of the symphony

Was there a "typical" symphony profile in the 1780s? By 1780, symphonies had long since abandoned the three-movement format that linked them to earlier Italian opera overtures. Haydn wrote no three-movement symphonies after 1765, while Mozart's "Prague" Symphony, with its famously absent Minuet, remains the exception that proves the rule.[34] The slow introduction, hardly a universal feature, came to dominate in Haydn's symphonies perhaps for two reasons: the increasing size of the forces and rooms for which he was writing (or the fact that he could only speculate about the sizes of rooms and orchestras in Paris and, before 1791, London); and the greater compositional choice in having quiet or off-tonic opening themes possible in the first movement once the big attention-getting gestures have played their part. Three of the six symphonies Mozart wrote after arriving in Vienna have a slow introduction – Nos. 36, 38, and 39.

Beyond its initial gesturing, the first movement of a symphony typically had an intelligible structure – a dramatic threefold division of material within two large sections (presentation of themes and keys, conflict, resolution) – and sufficient contrast in orchestration; the latter would often delineate the former. Recent studies on the level of understanding of Haydn's audiences suggest that concert-goers not only knew what to expect, formally speaking, but they also reveled in their own powers of enjoyment and understanding, and prized being able to recognize when conventions were being set aside.[35] In the slow movement, a greater diversity of pattern prevailed. After Haydn introduced the slow variation movement into the symphony (No. 47, 1772) and became celebrated for his style of orchestral variations, many other composers followed suit, although Mozart did not, finding sonata forms more congenial.[36] Other formal designs all stressed the pleasures of recognition as well: rondos and ternary (ABA) movements, sonata forms with and without development were all possibilities.

As for the minuet and trio, more members of the audience were likely to be familiar with this stereotype than any other: they played minuets at home, danced to them in the large and small ballrooms in Vienna (the Redoutensäle) or at other gatherings, studied music composition, which usually began with instruction in small forms, or simply attended other concerts.[37] It ought also to be noted that this was the only place on a concert program that a minuet would appear, since minuets were never part of concertos or the other genres to be performed; occasionally a concerto movement or aria might be in "Tempo di Menuet," but this was rare and became nonexistent. The most popular kinds of finales were very fast rondos, or quick sonata-form movements with the square, possibly binary-form themes of rondo style. Haydn and Mozart were assiduous in exploring the possibilities of hybrid forms combining sonata and rondo, although which composer did it first has been debated.[38] In general, the "weightier" movements in a symphony were the first two, although the balance among the movements began to change during the 1780s.

The broadest set of expectations the audience might have, however, had nothing to do with the specific tempos or formal attributes of the symphonies. Rather, in whatever concert venue, symphonies were expected to provide a certain kind of grand musical experience, to be stirring and exciting. These were not expectations anyone would have had for the intimate genres of the keyboard, such as sonatas and trios, or even for string quartets. Not only were symphonies discussed in terms of "grand" or "elevated" style, then, but this style was also differentiated from other less public genres.[39] As we will see in the next chapter, evoking the grand style raises a host of new issues.

2

Grand style and sublime in eighteenth-century aesthetics

The symphony occupied a prominent position in late-eighteenth-century discussions of aesthetics, genre, and form, for reasons that are not hard to discern. First, as we have seen, it had an inevitable part in musical life of the period, whether in concerts, in operas and oratorios, or in music performed in churches. Because the symphony had so many purposes, venues, and formal arrangements, critics and theorists could address a variety of rewarding subjects. Second, its "something-for-everyone" approach to instrumentation did not elicit the endless debates over the propriety of virtuosity that clouded the critical reception of concertos and soloists.[1] And finally, it came to occupy a position both grand and normative, by virtue of its scoring, its prominent mood-setting placement as the first (and often last) music heard, and its role in establishing and keeping before the public certain formal principles that could generate and then either satisfy or surprise audience expectations.

Symphony and elevated style

A significant discussion of the symphony from the early 1770s should put some of these assertions into perspective. J. A. P. Schulz, who wrote many of the music entries in Sulzer's influential encyclopedia *General Theory of the Fine Arts*, described the symphony this way:

The symphony is excellently suited for the expression of the grand, the festive, and the sublime. Its purpose is to prepare the listeners for an important musical work, or in a chamber concert to summon up all the splendor of instrumental music. If it is to satisfy this aim completely, and be a closely bound part of the opera or church music that it precedes, then besides being the expression of the grand and festive, it must have an additional quality that puts the listeners in the frame of mind required by the piece to come, and it must distinguish itself through the style of composition that makes it appropriate for the church or the theater.

The chamber symphony, which constitutes a whole in and for itself and has no following music in view, reaches its goal only through a full sounding, brilliant, and fiery style. The allegros of the best chamber symphonies contain great and bold ideas, free handling of composition, seeming disorder in the melody and harmony, strongly marked rhythms of different kinds, powerful bass melodies and unisons, concerting middle voices, free imitations, often a theme that is handled in the manner of a fugue, sudden transitions and digressions from one key to another . . . strong shadings of the forte and piano, and chiefly of the crescendo . . . Such an allegro is to the symphony what a Pindaric ode is to poetry. Like the ode, it lifts and stirs the soul of the listener and requires the same spirit, the same sublime power of imagination, and the same aesthetics in order to be happy therein . . . The andante or largo between the first and last allegro has indeed not nearly so fixed a character, but is often of pleasant, or pathetic, or sad expression. Yet it must have a style that is appropriate to the dignity of the symphony.[2]

Schulz's article was twice quoted by the astute theorist Koch nearly twenty and thirty years later, suggesting its staying power in the German-speaking orbit, just as Rousseau's dictionary of 1768 remained in the French one, being extensively quoted in the *Methodical Music Encyclopedia* of 1792–1818.[3]

The three terms by which Schulz initially characterizes the expressive purpose of the genre – "Ausdruck des Grossen, des Feyerlichen und Erhabenen," expression of the grand, the festive, and sublime – are richly suggestive for contextualizing the late Mozart symphonies, and for getting closer to the "Jupiter." Indeed, Mozart's first biographer, F. X. Niemetschek, described Mozart's late symphonies, especially the "Prague," as "full of surprising transitions and a fleet, fiery course, so that they immediately predispose the soul to the expectation of something sublime."[4] These terms not only place the symphony on a high, exalted stylistic level, but in referring to level at all also immediately invoke the authority of ancient texts. The rhetorical treatises of classical antiquity, such as those by Aristotle, Cicero, and Quintilian, distinguished among three stylistic "levels": the plain or low, the middle, and the elevated or grand.[5] A stylistic level would be chosen for a speech (or part of one) depending on context and purpose, because the plain style was held to instruct, the middle style to charm or conciliate, and the elevated style to move the passions of the audience.[6] In music, eighteenth-century writers like Mattheson, Scheibe, Forkel, and Schulz made the familiar distinctions among church, theater, and chamber styles; while these did not necessarily correspond to high, middle, and low, church style was the most consistently elevated simply because of the exalted feelings it was intended to produce. Forkel claimed that each style could have all three levels, depending upon whether the listeners were more or less educated.[7] The simultaneous difficulty and formality of the fugue suited it to church style, but it could be invoked at the higher end of the stylistic spectrum in any genre, like the symphony, as Schulz made clear.[8] In the general revaluing of instrumental music that emerged during the late eighteenth century, the symphony was generally considered the highest type, just as the ode was held to be the highest type of poetry.

Rhetoric in the late eighteenth century

In order to assess the role of the symphony in eighteenth-century thought, it first becomes necessary to place the symphony within a set of rhetorical concepts, the levels and venues of style, and consequently to establish the continuing importance of rhetoric to that period. Although rhetoric was no longer the vital force in public life and letters that it had been earlier in its long and venerable history, its influence was still pervasive in the eighteenth century.[9] Education in Germany and Austria, whether in *Gymnasium* or church school, continued to include the study of rhetoric: not only Leopold Mozart in Augsburg, but even Schiller and Hegel came under its sway.[10] Writers on music had since the sixteenth century invoked rhetoric as a model of composition, extemporizing, and evaluation.[11] Moreover, musical writers of the eighteenth century discussed rhetorical concepts in a pervasive, all-encompassing way: Mattheson, for example, discussed not only melodic invention but also musical structures from phrase to piece in terms of the parts of an oration; Scheibe argued that a rhetorical element was necessary even in instrumental music in order to draw in, please, and move the audience; Marpurg and Forkel asserted that rhetoric included virtually every aspect of musical composition and performance.[12]

Yet rhetorico-musical parallels have been tainted by their association with earlier labelling exercises – the enthusiastic application of figures and tropes to music by German theorists of the late sixteenth and seventeenth centuries that was taken up with equal enthusiasm by their musicological counterparts of the first half of the twentieth.[13] With the renewed interest in rhetoric in all fields since the late 1960s, and since the publication in 1980 of George Buelow's article on "Rhetoric and Music" in the *New Grove Dictionary* with its extensive tables of musico-rhetorical figures, more skeptical voices have emerged, notably Peter Williams and Brian Vickers.[14] It needs to be pointed out, however, that inappropriate musical analogues to rhetorical figures say more about the theorists who developed them than about the ultimate applicability of rhetoric to music.[15] Moreover, while rhetoric certainly includes the study of figures, it is by no means limited to that role.

11

The aspects of rhetoric to be adduced here are based principally, though not exclusively, on its broad network of ideas, because, as Vickers admonished, "In the study of rhetoric, as with all other disciplines, a narrow conception leads to narrow thinking, facile rejections, and hasty abandonment of the subject. Give rhetoric a trivial function and you trivialize it; conceive of it as widely as it originally existed, and you may begin to do justice to it."[16] The most fundamental of these aspects is that rhetorical modes of thought operated throughout the eighteenth century and were part of the "mind-set," as it were, not only of theorists but of Haydn and Mozart themselves, affecting the structure of their prose and even their occasionally articulated aesthetic principles. I have suggested elsewhere that Haydn's autobiographical sketch of 1776, supplied in letter form for publication in a book about notable Austrians, is a classic rhetorically organized composition, drawing particularly on the medieval *ars dictaminis*, the art of letter-writing, still current in manuals of the period: first an introduction (*exordium*), incorporating the so-called "securing of good-will" (*benevolentiae captatio*, in this case by self-deprecation); then the narration of facts (*narratio*, his biography); the supporting evidence (*corroboratio*, the list of his best-received pieces); the refutation of his enemies' arguments (*confutatio*, the Berlin critics); and the conclusion revealing again his good qualities as well as those whom he admires and respects (*peroratio*).[17]

Mozart's more formal letters also show just such a reliance on this approach. In fact, the most well-known letters to his Masonic brother Michael Puchberg written in 1788 and 1789 reveal not the frigidly stylized elements of *opera seria*, with which they were stigmatized by Wolfgang Hildesheimer, but rather the stylized effects of the *ars dictaminis*.[18] Indeed, this goes a long way toward explaining one of their more jarring effects, Mozart on his knees suddenly reverting to a practical tone. In the first lengthy plea, written before 17 June 1788, Mozart secures goodwill with "The conviction that you are *indeed my friend* and that you know me to be a *man of honour* encourages me to open my heart to you completely." His case, the request for a sizable amount of capital, proceeds by a list of the benefits of such a loan. Supporting evidence are his prospects for subscriptions and patrons, and the depth of responsibility of friendship and brotherhood; protestations of his means of economizing serve as an indirect refutation of arguments by enemies that he might have spendthrift habits; finally, the peroration expresses confidence and devotion. The long letter of 12 July 1789 is even more detailed in these respects, at once more heartrending ("poor sick wife and child") and factual ("Meanwhile I am composing six easy clavier sonatas for Princess Friederike"). That Puchberg was a Mason is significant: it seems more than likely that the rituals and formalized relationships of Freemasonry offered Mozart many opportunities for stylized discourse.[19] Certainly orations were part of lodge occasions, and one of the lodge officers was called the Orator.[20]

More specific rhetorical ideas drawing on the first three of the five parts of classical rhetoric (invention, arrangement, elaboration, memory, performance) will be discussed in Chapters 5 and 8, in conjunction with the first and last movements of the "Jupiter": musical topics, part of invention; the parts of an oration, subsumed under arrangement; and musical figures, part of style or elaboration. As we will see, topics and figures are closely associated with stylistic levels, and may act as signifiers of a particular "height" (the elevated style, for example) or a particular "place" (theater or church, for example), while arrangement affects the emotional responses of the audience. To identify symphonies as "grand" or "elevated," then, is to raise a host of rhetorically related questions. Moreover, to use the term "sublime" in descriptions of symphonies, as Schulz did, is to move beyond the conventional orbit of eighteenth-century music aesthetics, beyond rhetoric, and into a category of aesthetic experience that seems both self-evident and highly complex.

Beyond elevated style: the sublime

The sublime is an aesthetic category that usually appears as a component of the elevated or grand style of rhetoric. Quintilian asserted that the grand style transports the audience with irresistible persuasive force: "it is this force and impetuosity that Aristophanes compares to the thunderbolt."[21] When we hold today that a musical composition or painting is sublime, we usually refer to this quality of moving exaltation, akin to religious uplift. But the sublime came to the attention of the eighteenth century in a rhetorical guise, through the translation of a first-century Greek treatise, *On the Sublime*, a work of profoundly original literary criticism attributed to a certain Longinus (now thought to be a first-century work by an unknown author, sometimes referred to as Pseudo-Longinus to distinguish him from the more famous third-century rhetorician).[22] *On the Sublime* was invoked again and again in the eighteenth century to help explain the power of certain kinds of artistic experience, and became the origin or proximate source of several tropes of the sublime.

Longinus does not merely consider sublimity as a kind of high figurative mode of speech, but rather as "the echo of a noble mind."[23] This creation of equivalence between concept and creator had the effect in the eighteenth century of the artists themselves being called sublime, and Longinus was considered a representative of the sublime. As Pope wrote of him: "His own example strengthens all his laws,/He is himself the great sublime he draws."[24] There are five sources of sublimity, according to Longinus: the ability to form grand conceptions, the stimulus of powerful and inspired emotion, an appropriate use of figurative language, noble diction and imagery, and the arrangement (or disposition) of words in the speech leading to a total effect of dignity and elevation. The first two of these, the most important ones, are "largely innate," hence natural, while the last three are the product of art.[25] Yet the first two (forming grand conceptions and the stimulus of powerful emotion) are also part of the rhetorical art of invention (*inventio*), while the last three are part of the theory of style (*elocutio*).[26] Thus invention is natural, stylistic elaboration a learned process.

Part of what made Longinus attractive to the eighteenth century was his unique discussion of genius and inspiration; in George Kennedy's words, he gave neoclassical rhetorical criticism "the means to rise above pedantic rules of composition without contradicting" those rules. He also provided later writers with their principal images, for example his identification of the opening of Genesis as exemplary of the sublime.[27] After him, the sentence "And God said 'Let there be light'; and there was light" became the permanent touchstone of sublimity; after him, the thunderbolt as analogy to the effect of the sublime became a standard trope.

The other important inheritance of antiquity in the eighteenth-century interpretation of "sublime" was the Pindaric ode, which we have already seen compared to the Allegro of the symphony by J. A. P. Schulz. Pindar's surviving odes are mostly glorifications of victorious athletes and their families at the annual sport festivals held in ancient Greece; they were intended to be sung by a choir, and accompanied by Pindar's music (now lost) and dance. Not only did they "exalt *nobility* of every kind, social, physical, aesthetic, spiritual," but the experience of being swept along by their extraordinary energy and vividness was likened by Horace to "a torrent rushing down rain-swollen from the mountains, overrunning its banks, boiling and roaring. We feel its tremendous power, we are excited and exalted and overwhelmed by its speed and energy, it is useless to argue and analyse, we are swept away as soon as we begin to read."[28] Boileau described their "beautiful disorder."[29] Eighteenth-century German writers often placed Klopstock in this tradition, as exemplar of the highest poetic genre, and Mozart was compared with him.[30] These effects sound remarkably like Schulz's reference to the symphony's "great and bold ideas, free handling of composition, seeming disorder in the melody and harmony." It is possible that in our hectic, noise-ridden age, we have trouble imagining the potentially transporting effect of even relatively small massed instrumental forces in an eighteenth-century concert room. Not that there weren't listeners who put a negative slant on what have so far been described as positive virtues: William Jackson, organist of Exeter Cathedral, wrote in 1791 that "composers, to be grand and original, have poured forth such floods of nonsense, under the sublime idea of *being inspired*, that the present SYMPHONY bears the same relation to good music, as the ravings of a bedlamite do to sober sense."[31]

The "sublime style" and Mozart

Transport aside, elevated language and elevated style did not necessarily produce the sublime. In an acerbic paragraph in his *Lectures on Rhetoric and Belles-Lettres* (published in 1783 but based on lectures given in the 1750s and 60s),[32] Hugh Blair skewered "what is called the sublime style":

Persons are apt to imagine, that magnificent words, accumulated epithets, and a certain swelling kind of expression, by rising above what is usual or vulgar, contributes to, or even forms, the sublime. Nothing can be more false. In all the instances of sublime writing, which I have given, nothing of this kind appears. "God said, let there be light; and there was light." This is striking and sublime. But put it into what is commonly called the sublime style: "The sovereign arbiter of nature, by the potent energy of a single word, commanded the light to exist". . . The style indeed is raised, but the thought is fallen.[33]

Blair's disdain for a so-called sublime style different from true sublimity is manifested by Mozart in a letter to his father of 28 December 1782.[34] Having undertaken to set an ode by Michael Denis to music, Mozart finds his task difficult because of the overblown text: "The ode is sublime, beautiful, whatever you like – only – too exaggerated and bombastic for my delicate ears." Here Denis's poem was written in the "sublime style"; it is an extended apostrophe to Gibraltar and the British admiral Howe who rescued it from blockade; the poem contains in its eleven stanzas fully thirty-five exclamation points. Mozart, who had earlier expressed joy at the British rescue of Gibraltar – "I am an arch Englishman" – and was therefore interested in the subject, sketched the first three stanzas in a declamatory style, but never finished the piece.[35] His judgment shows that he was fully cognizant of current aesthetic speculation; indeed, in the same letter, Mozart expressed the desire to write a short book of music criticism with examples. For his part, Denis, who took on the persona of a heroic bard in his own poetry after he translated Ossian, was also a Jesuit, a Mason, and a professor who wrote a major treatise on rhetoric.[36]

Mozart's views of the "sublime style" versus what might be called "true sublimity" may have been affected in later years by Baron van Swieten and his championing of Handel's music; between 1788 and 1790, Mozart made "updated" arrangements of several large-scale works by Handel at van Swieten's request.[37] As van Swieten wrote to him in 1789, praising one aspect of Mozart's arrangement of *Messiah*: "He who is able to dress up Handel with such dignity and taste that he can on the one hand please even the dandies [*Modegecken*] and on the other hand nevertheless always display him in his sublimity, he has felt his value, he has understood him, he has attained the source of his expression."[38] Why was Handel's choral music considered sublime? Singled out were both its "monumental simplicity" and Handel's status as "the only great fughist exempt from pedantry," as Burney put it.[39] Mainwaring's biography quoted Robert Price on Handel: "in his sublime strokes, of which he has many, he acts as powerfully upon the most knowing as upon the ignorant."[40] Thus the sublime experience levels the distinction among listeners. And the unreliable Rochlitz even put these words in Mozart's mouth: "Handel knows better than any of us what will make an effect; when he chooses he strikes like a thunderbolt."[41]

It was van Swieten who suggested to Haydn that the words "And God said, 'Let there be light'; and there was light" be set only once in *The Creation*.[42] The result, perhaps the most celebrated moment in that celebrated piece, was a recognizable symbol of the sublime: Haydn's overpowering C-major tutti on the word "Licht," in its brevity, simplicity, sudden loudness, transition from darkness to overpowering light, and magnificence produces a sense of wonder and awe, transport and respect. In addition, it concludes with the Handelian suspension-laden cadence.

The sublime of terror

The influential formulation by Edmund Burke, in *A Philosophical Enquiry into the Origin of Our Ideas of the Sublime and Beautiful* (1757, enlarged two years later),[43] affords a larger picture of the impact of sublime experience; while not fully germane to symphonies, it is important for opera. Burke's treatise, dropped into a growing body of literature on beauty, the disinterested contemplation of which was essential to the formation of aesthetics in this period, powerfully described a sublime of the supernatural, dark, disordered, painful, terrifying sort:

16

Whatever is fitted in any sort to excite the ideas of pain, and danger, that is to say, whatever is in any sort terrible . . . is a source of the *sublime*; that is, it is productive of the strongest emotion which the mind is capable of feeling . . . In this case, the mind is so entirely filled with its object, that it cannot entertain any other, nor by consequence reason on that object that employs it. Hence arises the great power of the sublime, that far from being produced by them, it anticipates our reasonings, and hurries us on by an irresistible force. Astonishment . . . is the effect of the sublime in its highest degree; the inferior effects are admiration, reverence and respect.

. . . To make anything very terrible, obscurity seems in general to be necessary . . . Everyone will be sensible of this, who considers how greatly night adds to our dread . . . [In] Milton['s] . . . description of Death in the second book [of *Paradise Lost*] . . . all is dark, uncertain, confused, terrible, and sublime to the last degree.[44]

In Burke's discussion of beautiful objects, on the other hand, it is immediately apparent how beauty ranks on the scale of vital experiences: they inspire love, rather than admiration, because they are small and smooth, with gradual variation, delicacy, and a clear and bright color. In a particularly damning statement, Burke observes that "There is a wide difference between admiration and love. The sublime, which is the cause of the former, dwells on great objects, and terrible; the latter on small ones, and pleasing; we submit to what we admire, but we love what submits to us."[45]

Burke was at pains to point out that sublime terror is actually a source of aesthetic delight, but only when the terror is at a certain remove: one must not be in danger oneself. A raging storm at sea is not a sublime experience if one is in the boat. We may experience the terror-filled contemplation of violent Nature – with our own safety assured – in the panic of the crowd in *Idomeneo*, confronted with the power of a raging sea and a formidable sea-monster sent by the irate Neptune, toward the close of Act II. We are at a double remove here – the crowd observes, experiences terror, is actually in danger, while we merely listen in (and even then the crowd is on the stage rather than on the brink) – but the violence of their utterance may fill us with awe.

Supernatural elements could have the same effect, as Mozart was well aware. In the exchange of letters concerning *Idomeneo*, he upholds all of the sublime attributes described by Blair and Burke in his setting of the subterranean voice of Neptune near the end of the opera: Mozart wanted it short – he commented "If the speech of the ghost in *Hamlet* were not so long it would be more effective"[46] – and terrifyingly intense, to penetrate and to astonish. Even Leopold Mozart, in making suggestions for the setting, had urged that it open with a short "subterranean rumble" with the effect of an earthquake (*Erdbeben*, translated by Emily Anderson as "thunderbolt"!), so that the attention of the audience will be aroused, will swell, and will strain to the utmost.[47] Ultimately Mozart prevailed over the librettist Varesco. The original chatty text was cut to the bone, and Mozart's version of seventy bars was cut, first to thirty-one, then to a mere nine bars of awe-inspiring oracle, complete with the trombones emblematic of the underworld.[48]

Similarly, the graveyard scene in *Don Giovanni*, traversing virtually the same supernatural landscape, filled a contemporary reviewer with "horror": "Mozart seems to have learnt the language of ghosts from Shakespear. – A hollow, sepulchral tone seemed to rise from the earth; it was as though the shades of the departed were seen to issue from their resting-places."[49] Indeed, the laughter literally freezes on Don Giovanni's lips. And the second-act Finale to *Don Giovanni*, the devastating opening chords of which intensify almost unbearably the music of the overture by substituting the chord on which the Commendatore had been mortally wounded in the duel, illustrates perfectly the Burkean sublime.

Kant's sublime

By the mid-eighteenth century, then, the sublime was thought of not only in rhetorical terms but as an experience, and, moreover, one that embodied, as Lyotard puts it, a "contradictory feeling – pleasure and pain, joy and anxiety, exaltation and depression."[50] Not only did the sublime become psychologically complex, but it was evaluated as part of a comparison: beautiful and sublime; naive and sublime; sublime and grotesque; beautiful, sublime, and pictur-esque, and so on. As Ronald Paulson has recently written, "the sublime and the beautiful . . . were not just opposing categories; they became . . . a sequence: not just the great natural upheaval versus the quiet sunlit meadow . . . but the progression to be desired or demanded or regretted from one of these to the other."[51]

Such a progression, with its attendant contradictory feelings, is often discernible in contemporary reactions to Mozart's music, particularly because of its level of difficulty. Neal Zaslaw quotes several reports which attest to the demands on both players, especially wind players, and listeners, suggesting that Mozart's craft could be appreciated in small doses but that there was too much to take in.[52] Yet, the element of excess, of "too much to take in," is precisely the focus of Immanuel Kant's discussion of the sublime in his *Critique of Judgment*, published in 1790.

In his "Analytic of the Beautiful," Kant examined the ways in which beauty, understood as the feeling of pleasure derived from the form of an object, creates harmony in our faculties of sensibility and understanding. In the "Analytic of the Sublime," however, Kant revealed a critical conflict between imagination and reason. Because the sublime experience, based as it is upon formlessness, cannot be understood, it appeals to our faculty of reason, a superior faculty of cognition. In the words of Paul Guyer, it "makes demands upon the imagination which imagination cannot fulfill, it presents objects which seem to exceed the organizing capacities of mind."[53] The sublime does this in two ways – by magnitude or extent, or what Kant called the "mathematical sublime," and by power or force, the "might of nature," what Kant called the "dynamical sublime," based on Edmund Burke. The mind deals with this by ascribing such sublime qualities to the world but actually locating them in our rational being, since we are superior to nature: as Kant put it, *"the sublime is that, the mere ability to think which, shows a faculty of the mind surpassing every standard of Sense."*[54] Moreover, the sublime has an ethical component, because the feeling of awe which it produces is entirely congruent with the universal moral law with its "mingling of pleasure and pain, of resistance and freely willed submission."[55] Thus we no longer experience the disinterested pleasure of beauty, arising from qualities of beauty inhering in natural objects, but the supersensory realm, in that qualities of sublimity inhere in our minds, not in the objects themselves.[56]

In fact, Kant's most famous dictum – the peroration of the *Critique of Practical Reason* that was used as his epitaph and copied and underscored heavily by Beethoven – is entirely in the realm of the sublime: "Two things fill the mind with ever new and increasing admiration and awe, the more often and the more steadily we contemplate them: the starry heavens above me, and the moral law within me."[57] The precise variant of Kant's sublime embodied by "the starry heavens" is, of course, the mathematical sublime. We cannot count the stars. After all, he says "Nature is therefore sublime in those of its phenomena, whose intuition brings with it the Idea of their infinity."[58] Neil Hertz describes the mathematical sublime as a kind of "sheer cognitive exhaustion, the mind blocked not by the threat of an overwhelming force, but by the fear of losing count or of being reduced to nothing but counting . . . with no hope of bringing a long series or a vast scattering under some kind of conceptual unity. Kant describes a painful pause – a 'momentary checking of the vital powers' – followed by a compensatory positive movement, the mind's exultation in its own rational faculties, in its ability to think a totality that cannot be taken in through the senses."[59]

In short, the sublime became part of a sequence of events, even the enactment of a plot. Because, in Kant's words, "the mind feels itself *moved* in the representation of the Sublime in nature; whilst in aesthetical judgements about the Beautiful it is in *restful* contemplation,"[60] this sense of movement comes with a sense of progress toward a destination, and may be seen as teleological, as a series of "stages ending in unmistakable closure."[61] Appreciating infinity – the happy final state accorded by reason – comes only after the painful and chaotic failure of imagination and the senses.

It is my contention that both the rhetorical grand style and the transporting power of the sublime (the thunderbolt) are essential to an understanding of Mozart's late symphonies, just as the Burkean sublime echoes convincingly in his operas; and that the Kantian "mathematical" sublime is particularly relevant to the "Jupiter." These varieties of sublime will be taken up in Chapters 6 and 8.

3

The composition and reception of the "Jupiter" symphony

Leopold Mozart's death in May 1787 in effect deprived us of the details or at least the face-saving rationales of Mozart's faltering career in the late 1780s, the most problematic period of his years in Vienna. Without that correspondence, biographers have been forced to interpret relatively scanty evidence, leading to such theories as Hildesheimer's on Mozart's abandonment by the aristocracy after his operas about wicked aristocrats, or the more sober financial interpretations of Braunbehrens and the cultural reading of Steptoe.[1] Thus, contradictory and fragmentary evidence makes assessing the state of Mozart's career in 1788 somewhat problematic; on the whole, it seems to have been the first of three increasingly difficult and frustrating years, before his career was finally reinvigorated in 1791.

The state of Mozart's career in 1788

On the positive side, Mozart had just been made "k. k. Kammer-Kompositeur" at an annual salary of 800 gulden (7 December 1787),[2] and the Viennese premiere of *Don Giovanni* on 7 May 1788 netted him 225 gulden from the Emperor.[3] He led gala performances of C. P. E. Bach's oratorio *Die Auferstehung und Himmelfahrt Christi*, organized by Baron van Swieten, on 26 February and 4 March, with an "orchestra of eighty-six persons" at the homes of the nobility, and on 7 March at the Burgtheater.[4] At one of these concerts he may even have played his Piano Concerto, K. 537 ("Coronation"), as an entr'acte.[5] He entered thirty works and groups of works into his catalogue: twelve multi-movement instrumental works, including three piano trios; the Divertimento, K. 563; nine arias, including three for the Vienna *Don Giovanni*; seven sets of the dances required by his court position (including two groups of six and one group of twelve, for a total of twenty-nine); and two groups of vocal canons, the entries just after the "Jupiter" (one group of eight and one group of three). In addition to these, he completed his arrangement of Handel's *Acis and Galatea* in November, so that there are entries in every month. And Alan Tyson has shown that two movements of the B♭-major Piano Concerto, K. 595, were most likely written in the summer of 1788 as well.[6] To put these numbers into context, in 1787 he had entered twenty-one works, including *Don Giovanni*, six multi-movement instrumental works, nine Lieder, and the A-minor Rondo for piano; in 1789, he entered fifteen works, including four multi-movement works, six arias, two smaller works for piano, dances, and he was also working on *Così*, completed in January 1790. The scanty output of 1790 seems to reflect both the nadir of his career and illness, with just *five* works – *Così*, three string quartets, and a piece for flute-clock – and no compensatory flurry of performances.[7] The twenty-two works he entered in 1791 can be read as signs of his career taking off again, but may also have drained his strength and hastened his death.

Despite the prolific output of 1788, and at virtually the same time that he was writing his three extraordinary symphonies, Mozart also wrote the first of the series of heartrending letters to his Masonic brother Michael Puchberg, the rhetorical import of which was described in Chapter 2. Continuing until the year of his death, the letters implored him for money, and revealed Mozart's failed attempts to put together subscription lists for his compositions, the intrigues against him in Vienna, and the desperate situation of his household as landlords demanded money and he kept moving to cheaper lodgings. It is clear that the small but steady income from his court position (a position he immediately inflated to *Kapellmeister* in his correspondence) and the remuneration for *Don Giovanni* were by no means adequate in 1788 to maintain his family in comfortable circumstances, and other scholars have interpreted the evidence to suggest that Mozart's financial situation deteriorated as a result, variously, of gambling debts, household mismanagement by Constanze, or imprudent attempts to live like the highly-paid theatrical people and aristocrats with whom they socialized.[8] Of course, there was genuine illness that required treatment as well, the chemists, doctors, and spas referred to in several letters.

The letters to Puchberg loom large for another reason: after Leopold died Mozart simply wrote to very few people besides Puchberg and Constanze. Of the letters he wrote between 1788 and 1791, fully twenty-one, or one-third, are to Puchberg (four in each of 1788, 1789, and 1791, with more in 1790), and forty-eight are to his wife. The letter regarded as the second in the correspondence with Puchberg, "before 17 June 1788,"[9] actually reads as though it were the first, in its rhetorical formality, and air of broaching and justifying a departure in their relationship. In it, Mozart at first asked to be bankrolled to the tune of "one or two thousand gulden, at a suitable rate of interest" and offered a lengthy rationale in support of that amount, but by the end was pleading "If you should find it inconvenient to part with so large a sum at once [suggesting that Mozart knows already that he will be asking again and again], then I beg you to lend me until tomorrow at least *a couple of hundred gulden.*" In the previous letter, estimated at "June 1788," Mozart still owes Puchberg eight ducats, and he asks for another hundred "until next week, when my concerts in the Casino are to begin. By that time I shall certainly have received my subscription money [that is, for the three string quintets, K. 406/516b, 515, and 516]." In the letter of "before 17 June," however, Mozart writes "You need not be anxious about the subscription: I am now extending the time by a few months. I have hopes of finding more patrons *abroad* than *here*." The quintets were first offered on subscription in April 1788, then extended to January 1789; it seems not unlikely he expected the money because of the extension. Moreover, because the symphonies were very likely composed with the Casino concerts in mind, yet were not completed until 10 August, the concerts – which may or may not ever have come to pass – were probably planned for the fall at least, when the nobility would have returned from their summer estates. The "June 1788" letter, therefore, might well date from August.[10]

The summer of 1788 and composition of the "trilogy"

Nearly every one of Mozart's six Viennese symphonies had a hasty gestation. About the "Haffner," requested by his father for festivities involving the Haffner family in Salzburg at a particularly busy time in Mozart's early career in Vienna, Mozart wrote on 20 July 1782: "I am up to my eyes in work . . . and now you ask me to write a new symphony! How on earth can I do so? . . . I shall work as fast as possible and, as far as haste permits, I shall turn out good work."[11] That last statement is qualified on 31 July with "I am really unable to scribble off inferior stuff." He sent the first movement on 27 July (having had to turn out the C-minor Wind Serenade, K. 388 "in a great hurry"), and the last of the movements on 7 August, in a total of two-and-a-half weeks. When Mozart stopped at Linz on his way from Salzburg to Vienna the following year, he wrote on 31 October: "On Tuesday, November 4th, I am giving a concert in the theatre here and, as I have not a single symphony with me, I am writing a new one [the "Linz"] at breakneck speed, which must be finished by that time";[12] here the time span, since he arrived the previous day, is five days. The "Prague" Symphony, performed in that city in January 1787, was entered into his thematic catalogue on 6 December

1786, only two days after the C-major Piano Concerto, K. 503, the last of the twelve concertos of his intensive performing period 1784–6; both were probably intended for his four subscription concerts that winter "in the Casino" and it has been asserted that he played the concerto at one on 5 December.[13] And the final three symphonies, as is well known, were entered into Mozart's catalogue in the summer of 1788, the E♭-major on 25 June, the G-minor on 26 July, and the C-major on 10 August. They too were intended for a series of concerts "in the Casino," either the casino in the Trattnerhof or Philipp Otto's new casino in the Spiegelgasse.

If it took place, this concert series would have been Mozart's last. There is certainly no less evidence for it than for the Advent concerts of 1786: both are referred to in a letter, the 1786 concerts in a letter from Leopold to Nannerl describing the contents of a lost letter from Wolfgang, the 1788 series in the letter from Mozart to Puchberg. Possibly the more casual round of events in a casino made records less well preserved. Recent scholars have distanced themselves from the earlier widely-held view that Mozart never heard his last symphonies, a romanticized picture of the starving, suffering artist denied the fulfillment of having his finest instrumental creations performed in his presence. Zaslaw gives a careful account of possible occasions at which any of these works might have been performed.[14] Landon asserts that the Casino concerts in fact took place, citing as evidence the two tickets that Mozart actually sent to Puchberg; moreover, the alternate scoring for the G-minor Symphony – added clarinets and rewritten oboes – coincides with the personnel list for a concert by the Tonkünstler-Sozietät of 16–17 April 1791 at which a Mozart symphony was conducted by Salieri.[15]

Besides a local concert series, another plausible impetus for the rapid composition of three symphonies was Mozart's long-held plan to go to England; he surely knew that Haydn had written in 1782 a set of three symphonies, Nos. 76–8, for a planned (but aborted) trip to England in 1783. Mozart's longstanding interest in England was reinforced by friendly acquaintance with Nancy Storace (the first Susanna), her brother Stephen (a composer), the singer Michael Kelly, and Mozart's pupil Thomas Attwood (between fall 1785 and the beginning of 1787).[16] Two disgusted letters from Leopold to Nannerl give an outline of Mozart's original plan as well as his opinion of it. On 17 November 1786, Leopold was irate at the suggestion that he should care for Mozart's children in Salzburg while the Mozarts went on to England during the following Lent. And in early March 1787, Leopold had just squired around Salzburg the four English people just mentioned. He goes on:

as I had gathered, he wants to travel to England, but his pupil [Attwood] is first going to procure a definite engagement for him in London, I mean, a contract to compose an opera or a subscription concert, etc. Probably Madame Storace and the whole company had filled him with stories to the same effect and these people and his pupil must have been the first to give him the idea of accompanying them to England. But no doubt after I sent him a fatherly letter, saying that he would gain nothing by a journey in summer, as he would arrive in England at the wrong time, that he ought to have at least two thousand gulden in his pocket, and finally that, unless he had procured in advance some definite engagement in London, he would have to be prepared, no matter how clever he was, to be hard up at first at any rate, he has probably lost courage.[17]

Without paternal admonitions in 1788, the possibility of travel might have seemed attractive again. In any case, these symphonies must have come in handy on his German tour in 1789, as did the "Coronation" Concerto, K. 537.[18]

Haydn's three pre-London "London symphonies" raise the question of Mozart's familiarity with Haydn's symphonies, as well as the role of the canonical number three, which had not previously bound Mozart in symphonic composition. He had jotted down the themes of Haydn's Symphonies 75, 47, and 62 in 1784, probably considering them for inclusion in his concerts, since the leaf containing these themes includes an *Eingang* for the C-major Piano Concerto, K. 415.[19] He also boasted to his father, on 15 May 1784 as part of a warning not to trust music copyists because Haydn had had many symphonies pirated this way, that he actually owned copies of Haydn's three latest symphonies.[20] These may have been Nos. 76–8, advertised by Torricella in Vienna in July 1784; or, less likely, Hummel's 1781 edition of six Haydn symphonies (issued in three parts), including Nos. 75, 62, and 63.[21] There are several striking similarities in the variation movements by Haydn (the slow movements of 75, 47, and 63), and variation movements by Mozart in the same period;[22] curious as well is the resemblance between the Andante of No. 77 and Don Ottavio's aria "Il mio tesoro."

These groups of works point to another recent grouping, Haydn's two sets of three "Paris" Symphonies of 1785–6. Three were published by Artaria in Vienna in December 1787, those in C major (No. 82, "The Bear"), G minor (No. 83, "The Hen"), and E♭ major (No. 84).[23] Not only did Mozart's three echo these keys in reverse order, but both Symphonies in E♭ are the only ones of each group with a slow introduction; the Symphonies in C are the only ones with main themes incorporating a change of dynamics and topic (see Chapter 5); and the Symphonies in G minor are the only ones with continuous, pulsating, yet periodic themes. These similarities seem to be beyond coincidence.

Most recent writers dismiss the idea that the last three symphonies constitute a consciously planned "trilogy" on Mozart's part, outside of the probability that he intended to publish a group of three. Because twentieth-century concerts often feature thematic or genre-based programming, an evening devoted to these three symphonies, with their different characters and affective orientations, makes sense to us, as it did to Tovey.[24] But Mozart would not have planned a concert like that, and while he may have aimed for maximum variety, internal similarities may be no greater than those in any group of works in the same genre composed in close temporal proximity; compare the earlier Viennese symphonies, K. 200–2. As a set of three works in the same genre with highly individual characters, one thinks also of the C-major and G-minor String Quintets composed in 1787, to which Mozart added the quintet arrangement (K. 406/516b) of the earlier Wind Serenade in C minor, K. 388, for a subscription set of three works.[25] A composer may plan works with deliberate contrasts rather than affinities in mind, but that very contrast molds a popular perception that they were intended as a group of "individuals" or "embodied affects."

Abetting this view of related contrasts, so to speak, is the concept of "key characteristics," or the venerable view that each major and minor key contained an innate association with a given mood, affect, mental state, demeanor, or, since writers on the subject hardly ever agreed with one another, an association with several moods.[26] When three works in different keys and modes are assembled, the panorama of affects suggests a serious attempt both to describe and to appeal to many aspects of the human psyche. Ultimately, an attractively varied mixture of the "noble and ardent" key of "quiet majesty" and "love" (E♭ major),[27] the "discontented" "lament" of G minor, suited to "frenzy, despair, agitation,"[28] and "innocent" "happy cheerfulness" of the "grandiose, military, majestic" C major,[29] will create a sense that this particular exploration of affects was conceived as a totality, regardless of the lack of evidence for such an assertion.

Perhaps relevant to the choice of key of the "Jupiter" is Austria's war with the Turks, begun in February 1788. The Austrian tradition of grand C-major symphonies, scored for trumpets and drums, employing the fanfares and rhythmic gestures of the military, the throne, and even the church, since festive masses were scored the same way, has long been noted.[30] As Johann Pezzl, a member of Mozart's lodge and chronicler of Viennese affairs, wrote in 1788,

After a fifty-year truce, Austria has recently begun fresh hostilities with the Ottoman Empire. On 9 February 1788 the Austrian declaration of war was made formally known to the Divan in Istanbul, the Pasha of Belgrade and the various Turkish border officials in Bosnia, Serbia, Wallachia, Moldavia, etc.; next day fighting broke out in several places. The whole of Europe has turned its attention to this spectacle, in which parts of Asia and Africa are also involved.

Vienna more than anywhere else is closely involved in this affair. The activities of the Austrian army, and its fate, on the Turkish borders, are the leading topics of interest among the public . . . Austria has every reason to feel optimistic about the outcome of the present Turkish War . . . One less pleasant aspect of the Turkish War is that the size of a loaf of bread in Vienna has been reduced by more than half, and that items of food have become dearer in exactly the same ratio, because all supplies from Hungary have been stopped.[31]

Mozart had already written a "German War-Song," "Ich möchte wohl der kayser seyn," K. 539, in March for a singer's concert, while the piece completed the day after the "Jupiter" was a Lied, "Beym Auszug in das Feld," K. 552 ("Dem hohen Kaiser-Worte treu"). Ulïbïchev's words of 1843 seem to ring true:

One might believe that the Symphony in C had been designed to glorify some extraordinary event in the annals of the world, some exceedingly happy and ever to be remembered victory! The loud ringing pomp of the orchestra . . . decidedly denotes the joyfulness of victory as the ground character of the work.[32]

It would indeed be ironic if the last symphony Mozart wrote for his last concert series were inspired by the very conflict that was depleting the Treasury, drying up opportunities for performing for fiscally worried patrons, causing the absence, illness, and premature death of Joseph (and the accession of his unenlightened brother Leopold in 1790). Braunbehrens points out that theaters remained open, opera was still performed, but "even the richest families now had tight budgets and were less inclined to spend large sums on private concerts and recitals . . . more and more aristocrats disbanded their private orchestras as a result of political events."[33]

The autograph manuscript

When in the 1970s the autograph of the "Jupiter" Symphony was returned to Berlin from Poland, where it had been taken during the Second World War, it was quickly issued in an attractive facsimile edition that far surpassed the facsimile edition of 1923.[34] Occasionally betraying signs of haste (the G-minor had been completed two weeks before), with squeezed, slanted inner-part figuration, the autograph is for the most part cleanly written, with just a few changes. The last two movements are especially error-free. It is likely that Mozart worked out the finale first in sketches, then made a fair copy; the folios are renumbered from 1. Mozart wrote the violin and bass parts first, as was his custom, then filled in the other voices; this can clearly be seen in crossed out bars containing only violin and bass (f. 5). Violins and violas are at the top two staves, then winds and brass, with cellos and basses at the lowest staff. The only major structural change occurred at the end of the second movement; the autograph shows that the return to the first theme (*a*) was an afterthought; because of the foliation we can see that he changed his mind after writing the minuet and trio. Moreover we can see his attention to detail in the figuration in the penultimate bar: the flute and violin were originally to repeat the figure played by the violin in the previous bar, but Mozart changed it to begin a third higher, thus including the ninth of the dominant chord and a bigger final leap. Considerations of shape made the final choice the more expressive one. There is also a change in figuration during the descent after the C-minor episode in the exposition of the first movement, bars 92–3. The original descent did not have the turning figure of bar 92 nor the *Eine kleine Nachtmusik* flavor of bar 93. A final alteration concerns the second theme of the first movement, which was possibly revised; the original, not extant, was replaced with a new bifolium.[35]

Reception and interpretation of the "Jupiter"

The majority of responses to the "Jupiter" Symphony have ranged from admiring to adulatory, a gamut from A to A; there were notable dissenting voices objecting to its "out-of-date" quality, or its confusion, but willing to admire it as a "formal model."[36] What is interesting in the array of biographers, critics, theorists, and composers is the spectrum of what might be called their discourse of approbation: acceptance of a canonized masterwork, enthusiastic explanation of its workings, degree of interest in the fugue, simple *Begeisterung*, celebration of its clarity, description of a transporting, bewildering epiphany. Affected by the changing image of Mozart and, in the nineteenth century, by their relationship to the pre-Beethovenian past, these writers often find it impossible not to compare the C-major with the G-minor, with unsurprising results. Sometimes we must guess that the C-major Symphony at issue is the "Jupiter." For example, E. L. Gerber, in his *Neues historisch-biographisches Lexikon der Tonkünstler* (1812–14), states that even if we knew but one of his noble symphonies (one quartet, etc.), like the "overpoweringly great, fiery, artistic, pathetic, sublime symphony in C . . . we would already have to perceive him as one of the first[-ranked] geniuses of modern times and the century just past."[37] It seems more than likely that such a description refers to the "Jupiter."

Similar terms were used by Nissen, Constanze's second husband and author of the first Mozart biography to be based on extensive documentary and anecdotal evidence. In a supplement to the biography dealing exclusively with the works, he actually said rather little about individual symphonies, mentioning only the last three. Of the "Jupiter," he wrote: "His great Symphony in C with the closing fugue is truly the first of all symphonies. In no work of this kind does the divine spark of genius shine more brightly and beautifully. All is heavenly harmony, whose tones, like a great noble deed, speak to the heart and enrapture it; all is the most sublime art, before whose power the spirit bows and is amazed."[38]

On the other hand, "F . . . ," a correspondent of the *Allgemeine musikalische Zeitung* in 1798, criticized the overenthusiastic imitators of Haydn and Mozart who made one tire of what might otherwise be wonderful compositional devices. In so doing, he gave qualified praise for the "Jupiter": "Haydn, in one of his newest and finest symphonies in C major [No. 95], had a fugue as a final movement; Mozart did this too in his formidable Symphony in C major, in which, as is well known, he came on a little too strong."[39]

Gernot Gruber, who charts the changing fortunes of Mozart's artistic reputation in *Mozart und die Nachwelt*, identifies 1830 as a turning point, when Mozart was relegated from a vital, valued presence in music to a more background figure.[40] Conflating ideas of musical progress, the threesome of Viennese Classicism, and the ratification of a Classic–Romantic split is this statement from the writer W. R. Griepenkerl: "Haydn is the creator, the root [of the triad], Mozart is the beautiful third, Beethoven the powerful fifth which impetuously rushes beyond to all regions."[41] Mendelssohn and Wagner modelled youthful symphonies on the "Jupiter."[42] But it was the performances of Mozart's works, especially by Mendelssohn, that "served to strengthen and confirm Mozart's canonization in the classical school."[43] Some reviews of these performances elicited comments about the "Jupiter," from the laconic "the immortal model and ideal of all symphonies" to remarks both more effusive and more detailed, as this one from the *Allgemeine musikalische Zeitung* of 1846:

How pure and clear [are] all the images within! no more and no less than that which each requires according to its nature. Recent music, in opposition to this principle, inclines here and there toward mysticism. It adds something extra, beyond what the ideas [themselves] prepare; it willingly envelops them in a harmonious fog. In the last movement, four themes are worked out. But to count is also to discover. It simply must be done only by a musical sensibility and not by a numerical sensibility. The ideas used in the piece [given in an example] are first sought one after another, and then explored each in itself. Then relationships such as [the strettos in second theme and development] and all the diversity which they develop later in the piece do not produce contingency but rather demand that the intellect must reckon up everything. Here is revealed how the master first collects his material separately, then explores how everything can proceed from it, and finally builds and elaborates [upon it]. That even *Beethoven* worked this way is revealed in his sketchbooks.[44]

It is striking to read that the thematic presentation and intricate contrapuntal procedures of the "Jupiter" are comparable to the compositional process itself, embodied in the final version of a piece. Interestingly, a much earlier reviewer of the *Eroica* wished for the "light, clarity, and unity" of the "Jupiter," characteristics shared by the G-minor Symphony, Beethoven's First and Second, and Eberl's E♭ and D-major Symphonies, to be introduced into the *Eroica*.[45]

Schumann and Brahms, in brief references, seemed to echo the "Jupiter"-as-immortal-model school of thought. Appearing to counter the purely intellectual pleasure just described in dealing with the piece, Schumann wrote

As a pedagogue, I must search for three objects – root, flower, and fruit; or for the poetical, the harmonic-melodic, and the technical content; or for the gain offered to heart, ear, and hand. Many works are wholly above discussion; for instance, Mozart's C major Symphony with Fugue, many works by Shakespeare, some of Beethoven's. Those, however, which are principally intellectual, individually characteristic, or stamped with mannerism give us cause to ponder.[46]

Presumably Schumann meant to imply that the "Jupiter" unites the three triple objects of his search, but one wonders about his relationship to such a work. Brahms's remark was merely a corrective to the view that Beethoven was more significant than Mozart; he said to Heuberger in 1896,

The attraction of novelty must be differentiated from inner value . . . I am able to understand too, that Beethoven's First Symphony did impress people colossally. In fact, it was the new outlook! But the last three symphonies by Mozart are much more important! Some people are beginning to feel that now.[47]

The remedy had already begun, because at the one-hundredth anniversary of Mozart's death, the most frequently performed works were the "Jupiter" and the *Requiem*.[48]

Coincidentally, the two most significant and extensive treatments of the "Jupiter" in the nineteenth century appeared in the same year, 1843, yet were diametrically opposed in approach. The poetic and descriptive side was represented by the *Nouvelle Biographie de Mozart* of 1843 by Aleksandr Ulïbïchev (1794–1858; Oulibicheff in French), a Russian aristocrat and art-lover; his rendering of the piece was subsequently translated from a German version into English in a Boston newspaper, *Dwight's Journal of Music*, in 1867, and has been included here as the Appendix because of its many beauties.[49] The analytical and technical side, on the other hand, is exemplified by the analysis of the "Jupiter" finale by Simon Sechter (1788–1867), which appeared as the appendix to the third edition of Marpurg's *Abhandlung von der Fuge* (1753–4).[50]

Ulïbïchev begins with an invocation of the Sublime:

The man of all kinds, all expressions, all contrasts, has bequeathed to us a last work, in which, instead of the elegiac ode (Symph. in G minor) with its most sorrowful outpourings, we find the Dithyramb raised to the highest pitch of splendor, of enthusiasm, of sublime Pindaric intoxication and bewilderment.

And his discussion of the Finale is again concerned not only with style but with the effect of the artwork:

Who could count the abominations which the learned ones of that day might have found in the Finale to the Symphony in C? How the fearful fugue with its four subjects must have heated their poor brains! This was neither BACH nor HANDEL, it was none of their acquaintance; it was MOZART. Where could they have found a measure for him, who had shattered their square and compass? Some of their criticisms have come down to us as monuments of their confusion . . . the free fugue of Mozart . . . does not subject itself to the methodical periods of the class and admits mixture of style . . . The fugue is no longer the mere abstract expression of some sort of emotion; it can become picture, translate itself into action, paint a battle or anything that is positive, without any danger of falling into that kind of music which requires a programme.

The most suggestive part of the discussion is his comparison of the function of the Finale vis-à-vis the symphony as a whole: he asserts that it is equal to the "emerging of order out of Chaos," with which Haydn's *Creation* begins, and that neither the fugues nor the melodic portions of the movement that use the same themes can be understood without the other. Ulïbïchev thus strikingly conflates images of the sublime with the complementarity of the galant and learned styles.[51] Saint-Foix was lavish in his praise of Ulïbïchev: "Berlioz apart, music had never, I believe, been previously spoken of in like terms."[52]

Sechter's much less eloquent remarks prepare a detailed analysis of the score, which he annotated with letters:

This is a work which in terms of skill and taste can enter the lists alongside any composition in the world. Its greatest perfection is its effortless fusion of free composition with strict, this being an art of which Mozart had full command. It therefore behooves every music-lover to become acquainted with the way in which Mozart's thought processes evolved [*Ideengang*]. Without doubt, his first conception [*Idee*] was to fashion an artistic product the elaborateness of whose deployment should not be foreseeable at its outset. The five themes that combine contrapuntally in the final section must unquestionably have been worked together in counterpoint right from the start. Only after that did he begin to develop each theme in its own right, unfolding the various delightful features of each one individually.[53]

Sechter's less than overheated language stands in stark contrast to the poetic Ulïbïchev. Even Sechter's conclusion, after an analysis that recognizes both the "demands" of sonata form (which he calls "symphony form") and the imitative treatment of both motives and orchestral instruments, casts the discourse in terms of audience "excitement" rather than sublimity and "bewilderment":

Mozart has given us here, as in so many of his works, proof positive that counterpoint, fugue and canon, far from being the sole preserve of solemn music, can also be used with excellent effect in light-hearted compositions. That he succeeded in this purpose can be deduced easily from the fact that at virtually every performance, this movement, despite its quite considerable duration, has had to be repeated, because even those who were not connoisseurs were greatly excited by it.

It is interesting to learn that a movement of a symphony over fifty years old could call forth such an audience response. Moreover, Sechter's reference to "light-hearted" versus "solemn" composition seems a ghost both of the stylistic levels of rhetoric and of the church, theater, and chamber styles, while his differentiation between members of the audience with more or less learning echoes the eighteenth-century distinction between *Kenner* and *Liebhaber*.

The other lengthy nineteenth-century analysis of the Finale appeared in a composition manual written by J. C. Lobe (1797–1881) in 1860. Offering the same kind of detailed contrapuntal examination as Sechter, and drawing on Sechter's work, he described the "free quintuple-fugue" as a "model of contrapuntal art that has not yet been equaled." He was especially careful to separate canon from fugue in his discussion. And, like Sechter, he pointed out that laymen would be just as delighted and swept away as the connoisseurs because of the power of the ideas, grace of the melodies, and splendor of the orchestration. And he concludes with the same kind of synthesizing statement that "all the charms of instrumental music are united," the "most serious strict counterpoint alternating with the most delightful homophonic melodies."[54]

With the lengthy account of this work in Abert's thoroughgoing revision of Otto Jahn's seminal *W. A. Mozart*, the kind of stylistic discussion common to twentieth-century biographical literature emerges.[55] Resemblances to other works are offered, the historical significance of motivic elements explored, the affective significance of instrumentation and modulations suggested: for example, of the retransition in the first movement (bars 183–8), Abert wrote "Bassoons and oboes show themselves inclined to revive the old contrapuntal round-dance – one of the most humorous spots in Mozart's symphonies – but the force of the organ point soon draws it back to the reprise."[56] Abert also points out that the theme of the slow movement is a "favorite idea" ("Lieblingsgedanke") of the era, identifying the same pattern in the middle movements of Haydn's sonatas Hob. XVI:35, 38, and 39, and in the finale of Beethoven's Fifth Symphony. Similarly, he includes the outline of the second theme of the Finale ($d^2b^1e^2f\#^1$) in the tradition of what Warren Kirkendale calls the "pathotype" fugue subject (normally in minor with a descending diminished seventh), and that includes the "eleison" motive of the "Kyrie" from Mozart's *Requiem*.[57]

To Tovey belongs, as usual, the witty encapsulation of a keenly observed truth. In his programme note to the "Jupiter," he compared the generic aspect of its themes to its two companion symphonies:

One of the most significant differences between Mozart's last three symphonies concerns the characters of their themes. In the E flat Symphony the themes are evenly poised between formulas on the one hand and attractive melodies on the other, with euphony always paramount. In the G minor Symphony almost every theme is highly individual and, even when formal in phrasing, quite unexpected in its course. In the last symphony we reach what is really the final subtlety of an immensely experienced artist, such as the god-beloved Mozart of the *Magic Flute* or the octogenarian Verdi of *Falstaff*. Most of the themes are not only formal, but are actual formulas. There are people who mistake this for a failure to achieve originality. They, as Mark Twain pointed out, whistle or hum the melodies during operatic performances, to show their culture, "and their funerals do not occur often enough."[58]

Perhaps a popular view of the conventionality of some of Mozart's materials, as well as the "Wagnerian movement," accounted for the falling-off of his popularity in the second half of the nineteenth century noted by Saint-Foix and Staehelin. Yet Saint-Foix reminds us that Wagner in his writings "has revealed himself as the most ardent and comprehensive protagonist of Mozart's three great symphonies."[59] Saint-Foix's own stylistic *aperçus* are rendered with great charm. He ends his description with this tribute:

with not the slightest risk of self-deception, we can say that nothing so great and important had arisen before that which dawned on August 10, 1788; neither in the orchestra nor in any chamber-music center had a comparable work been heard. And now behold Mozart with his bold felicity, for what reason we know not, raising up this brilliant edifice and crowning it with a vast instrumental "chorus" that saw the older music, suddenly revived, united with the new to salute the future! With a sovereign grace, eloquence, and force, the master in his thirty-second year gathers up all the elements his most glorious predecessors have used and reveals to us all that music has achieved up to his time, and what it will do nearly a hundred years later. That such a work should have proved too difficult for some hearers need not surprise us.[60]

Alfred Einstein's important discussion of the "fusion of *galant* and 'learned' styles" that he found particularly compelling in Mozart's late style, and which is "complete" in the "Jupiter" finale, has been influential in forming a general view of Mozart's music.[61] Identifying the contrapuntal as the most serious element in music to Mozart, Einstein suggested that he reconceived the symphonic style in this light, that Mozart imagined the symphony to be not mere curtain-raiser, but "the very center of a concert program." Subsequently the term "galant" itself has been studied and struggled with.[62]

A host of specialized studies largely concerned with the Finale were published between the 1950s and the 1980s that brought source-critical and analytical issues to the fore. Johann Nepomuk David sought to reveal that the first ten notes of the Finale played by the first violin ($\hat{1}$–$\hat{2}$–$\hat{4}$–$\hat{3}$–$\hat{6}$–$\hat{5}$–$\hat{4}$–$\hat{3}$–$\hat{2}$–$\hat{1}$ or c–d–f–e–a–g–f–e–d–c) formed a common thematic substratum to all the movements of the work; he stated categorically "The Jupiter Symphony rests on a cantus firmus (c.f.) of ten notes, from which every main and subsidiary theme, every transition and coda of the entire work unfolds."[63] That the first four notes alone continued to exert fascination after King published a list of works in which that subject appears[64] is attested by the variety of studies examining or analyzing its treatment. Ellwood Derr offers "with conviction" a cantus firmus from Fux's *Gradus ad Parnassum* as Mozart's "source," and analyzes all of the appearances of the motive in Mozart's music, concluding that the "Jupiter" Finale represents the fulfillment of all the tendencies in its earlier appearances.[65] Gerd Sievers's detailed analysis of the Finale made frequent reference to the nineteenth-century analyses by Sechter and Lobe; its interesting conclusion is that within each of the conventional sonata-form sections (exposition, etc., including the coda) exists a miniature sonata-form pattern – the exposition *per se* even has two of these – comprising "exposition" with two different "themes," a period of working-out similar to "development," then a "reprise" of one or both of the themes in that section.[66] For example, using the theme-designations in the diagram of this movement in Chapter 4, the first group of the exposition (bars 1–73) contains an exposition (1a–1b, bars 1–35), a development of 1a, bars 36–56, and a reprise of 1b, bars 56–73.

Susan Wollenberg, noting that "theme-tracing is a pastime with which musicians can become dangerously obsessed," reveals the historical tradition of Viennese keyboard practice concerning the subject of the Finale, and concludes that the subject takes the first four notes of the hymn *Lucis creator*.[67] One of the intriguing threads traced by Katharine Thomson in *The Masonic Thread in Mozart* is the relationship between imitative counterpoint and Masonic ideals of equality and brotherhood; she places the "Jupiter" finale in this context.[68] Moreover, she suggests that the contrasting themes used in the finale's fugue indicate that the piece embodies the Pythagorean ideal of the fusion of opposites in the mean, an idea admired by Freemasonry. But then she goes a bit far in finding the last three symphonies to be a Masonic trilogy in significant keys: an apprentice knocking three times at the door in the first movement, many elements similar to *Die Zauberflöte*, the aspirations of the common people represented by the popular-style theme at the end of the exposition: in short, the symphony as an expression of some of Mozart's "profoundest ideas in perfect form."[69] Much interesting material on Mozart and Masonry has recently been brought to light by Philippe A. Autexier,[70] and although investigating Masonry tends to make one see it everywhere, I believe there is still more to be done with it in the "Jupiter." One thread the work of Wollenberg and Thomson suggests is the idea of light. Thomson identified C major as the "key of Light," and believes the "Jupiter" to embody Masonic ideals. Wollenberg identified *Lucis creator*, which means "creator of light." Moreover, in the Song of the Salii (the Salian priests in Rome), Jupiter "figures as a state deity, and is addressed as Lucetius, the God of Light."[71] To complete this speculative interlude, Salomon, who probably named the symphony, was a Mason.[72] Connections between Salomon, who tried to get Mozart to come to England in 1790, Mozart, and Haydn have yet to be explored in the context of Masonry and its meanings.

The most recent scholarly discussions of the "Jupiter" reveal new interpretive stances, and have already aroused controversy.[73] In Neal Zaslaw's magisterial, and highly source-oriented book, the last chapter speculates on possible "meanings for Mozart's symphonies," with the "Jupiter" receiving the sole extended exploration.[74] Surveying the heterogeneous, disturbing, and complex elements of the work, culminating in a finale that "transcended the boundaries of the genre as it was then understood," Zaslaw develops a daring "plot" for the whole that hinges on a social and political interpretation. The characters of opera *semiseria* in the first movement join with the "liturgical tag" of the Finale that Mozart had used for the words "Credo, credo" in his Missa brevis in F major, K. 192/186f, to create a kind of manifesto of social equality and a defiant over-complication of a style his contemporaries already found too difficult. As support for his assertions of some of the more difficult aspects of Mozart's style, he adduces an article by Rose Rosengard Subotnik that identifies the "irrational elements" in Mozart's late symphonies as heralding a breakdown in commonly accepted views of reason "as a universally unified and grounded structure" in favor of a "far more problematical notion of rationality as an individually or culturally particular vision."[75] The monograph by Stefan Kunze, largely a detailed analysis, has a fascinating final chapter, in which he suggests that counterpoint and fugue in the music of Classical composers should not be viewed as an evocation of *stile antico* or as part of the reception history of older music, but rather as a new arena of compositional activity that must be taken on its own terms.[76]

4

Design: four movement-plans

In providing a general outline of each movement, with charts and musical examples, this chapter aims to be a convenient summary of the symphony as a whole to which the reader may refer in following the more specific local arguments in the next four chapters. The examples are keyed to the tables.

Movement 1: Allegro vivace   (Table 4.1. and Example 4.1). A fully elaborated sonata form with clearly articulated divisions, this movement adumbrates elements of the second, third, and fourth movements (textures, metrical ambiguities, registral oppositions, harmonic interjections beginning in C minor). It also embodies a dramatic movement from the grand style of the opening theme to the thin-textured lyricism of the second theme, to the accessible, more popular and even folk-oriented closing theme. Yet it is the closing theme that generates the development. To resolve this progression is one of the tasks of the finale.

It is not necessary to indulge in minute thematic-resemblance hunts in order to appreciate the significance of elements of the first movement that appear in subsequent parts of the symphony. They are, in order of appearance in the first movement:

1 Tutti portion of opening theme, leading to half cadence, followed by soft reiteration of opening theme: same in finale.

2 C-minor interjection at end of second group, bar 81: sudden C-minor outburst in second movement at beginning of transition (bar 19); a C-minor episode occurs in closing group of finale (bar 127); in addition, corresponding spots in recapitulations of first movement and finale both begin in F minor and go up to D♭ major.

3 Second theme, bars 56, 244: texture recurs at beginning of minuet and at beginning of finale (first theme); moreover, the imitation in the bass of second theme also appears in finale.

37

4 Development section, dissonant ascending progression with chromatic bass line, on C–D–E, bar 171; in recapitulation of finale, after first theme there is a dissonant progression of C–D–E–D–C with chromatic wind line (bar 233).

Movement 2: Andante cantabile (Table 4.2 and Example 4.2). In this slender sonata-form movement of only just over one hundred bars, Mozart compresses a maximum of lyric grace and emotional striving. There were few constraints either of key or of form for the slow movement in this period. Mozart favored some kind of sonata-form design for the majority of his slow movements, occasionally choosing rondo or ternary (ABA) form instead, or feinting in that direction with a closed theme in binary form (two-reprise form, in eighteenth-century parlance). Often the development of themes or harmonies is delayed until the recapitulation in the so-called "sonatina form" or "sonata form without development," an unhappy term which makes it appear, in Leo Treitler's words, as though "the *absence* of a development is a salient point in the work's unfolding."[1] An interesting distinction between the musical personalities of Haydn and Mozart can be observed here: most of Haydn's symphonic slow movements are in sonata form up to the mid-1770s. By 1780 nearly every one of them is more sectionally divided, either as a variation movement, a rondo-variation, or an alternating variation, with a few other unusual sectional hybrid forms thrown in for good measure, including combinations of sonata, rondo, and variation. Mozart, on the other hand, seemed to prefer a sonata format above all, and wrote no variation movements whatsoever in his symphonies, and only three slow variation movements in the piano concertos (K. 450, 456, and 482, the last of them a rondo-variation).[2]

Movement 3: Menuetto, Allegretto (Table 4.3 and Example 4.3). By the late eighteenth century, the minuet and trio were a virtually inevitable part of any symphony, with a virtually inevitable formal pattern: a binary (two-reprise) form minuet followed by a different binary form known as the trio. Within the small dimensions of the movement, however, composers often "played against type" or otherwise exploited audience expectations of a typical pattern. And by keeping the trio in the tonic, as he does here, Mozart can play with other conventions, as in the trick of beginning with a "final cadence." The latest research shows that when the minuet was repeated after the trio, its repeats would most likely be observed, in contrast to most recorded versions but as is done on some with eighteenth-century instruments.[3]

Movement 4: Finale. Molto allegro   (Tables 4.4–4.5 and Examples 4.4–4.5).
In German-speaking countries the symphony has been commonly referred to
as the C-major Symphony "mit dem Schlussfuge," and nearly all commentators have been at pains to point out that the last movement is not actually
a fugue but rather a sonata form with fugal portions. Plausibly viewed as the
culmination of the entire work – perhaps the first finale-driven symphony –
it contains an extraordinary amount of counterpoint: fugato, canon, and
imitation of motives in a developmental sense. Canon and imitation are found
in every section of the movement, fugato in the first group and in the coda.
Mozart specified a second-half repeat here, as he did in the finales of the two
other symphonies of 1788, though not in the "Prague," "Linz," or "Haffner."
It is not surprising that writers have tended to use the word "apotheosis" when
discussing this movement. The five musical ideas of the piece, combined in
the fugato and canon of the coda, are shown combined in Example 4.5, which
comes from the analytical accounts by Sechter and Lobe (see Chapter 3).

   In the charts that follow, I have used the arabic numbers 1 and 2 for first
group and second group, respectively, modified with letters a, b, c, for
different thematic segments (1a, 2b); letters m, n, p, q refer to phrase
structures; letters w, x, y, z refer to motives; the abbreviation **Br.** for the
"bridge passage" that modulates to the dominant in the exposition (and its
return with modifications in the recapitulation),[4] and the abbreviation **Cl.** for
closing group.[5] Other abbreviations: retrans. = retransition; ext. = extension;
mod. = modulation; diss. = dissonant; chrom. = chromatic[ism]; seq. =
sequence; G. P. = General Pause; cir/5 = circle of fifths; E = E major,
Em = E minor, E/m = E major/minor. In the finale, I have used capital **A**
and **B** to identify the bifurcated parts of each functional area. I have tried to
balance ease of chart-reading with completeness of information. Bar numbers
are given in the second column after the functional area.

Table 4.1. *"Jupiter" Symphony, I: Allegro vivace, C major, C time, 313 bars*

EXPOSITION, bars 1–120

First group (tonic)

1a	1	"grand style"
		x (f) + y (p) (2+2 + 2+2)
	9	fanfare (f) on inverted x (to fermata)

First group/bridge passage

1b–	24	x (p) + y (p) with w (fl./ob. countermelody)
Br.		ext. of y (mod. begins; rests of 1a filled in with countermel. and elisions)
	37	x (f) + y (f) with w + ext. on y (holes filled in)
	49	fanfare (to rest)

Second group (dominant)

2a	56	"singing style"
		m (6_V) + m ($6/$ + $4m$ ext$_I$) + n (4_I + $4_{V/V}$) (y in bass connects m + m), two phrases of n), to G. P.
2b	81	C-minor "shock"/C major
2c	89	tutti on y (quasi-closing theme)
		6 + 6 (elided) + 2 (trans.)

Closing (dominant)

Cl.a	101	popular-style theme (from opera aria); elided, repetitious
		tail = z^1 + z^2 (from y)
Cl.b	111	tutti (to *Eine kleine Nachtmusik* cadence)
	117	fanfare

DEVELOPMENT, bars 121–88

121	wind trans. (cf. Sym. 40/I, Beeth. Sym. 1/I)
124	**Cl.a** in E♭
133	tail of **Cl.a** (=z^2); E♭–Fm–Gm–Fm–E♭–Gm–Dm–Am (+antiphonal winds)
155	"false retrans."
161	"false reprise-interlude" on **1b** (w in bsn.): F major
	x (p)+ y (p), seq. on x + w
171	tutti: seq. on x + inverted x; Am–E/m–D/m–C/m–V
181	tail of **Cl.a**, first str., then (articulating retrans.), in winds with sustained horns, to desc. scale

RECAPITULATION, bars 189–313

First group (tonic)

1a	189	x (f) + y (p)
	197	fanfare

Bridge passage

1b–	212	x (p) + y (p) with w in Cm–E♭
Br.	220	desc. sequential ext. on y to aug. 6
	225	x (f) + y (p) with w + ext. on y
	237	fanfare

Table 4.1 (*cont.*)

Second group (tonic)

2a	244	**m + m + n**, to G. P.
2b	269	F minor/D♭ major "shock" (cf. finale)
2c	277	tutti on **y**, quasi-closing theme

Closing (tonic)

Cl.a	289	$z^1 + z^2$
Cl.b	299	with wide leaps
	306	fanfare with 5-bar ext. of last chord

Example 4.1.   Mozart, K. 551/I, themes and motives

41

Table 4.2. *"Jupiter" Symphony, II: Andante cantabile,*
F major, $\frac{3}{4}$, 101 bars, violins con sordini

EXPOSITION, bars 1–44

First group (tonic)

1   1   **a** 4 (2 + 2) + 2 [cadence denied, needed short consequent] + 5
            (ornate, with 32nds)

      11   **a** in bass, now answered by 32nds, 2 + 2 + 4
            (no preparation)

Bridge passage

Br.   19   **b** C minor "shock"; ob./bsn. upbeat, *fp*, sync. strings with offbeat
            16th triplets (appoggiaturas); 2 + 2 + 5 (shock bars telescoped
            to 2 beats long from 3 beats, so heard 5 times)

Second group (dominant)

2   28   C maj.: $2_V + 2_I + 3_V$ (cir/5) + 5_I (imit. in fl.; ext. into seq.
            through flat side, on turning figure [quasi-z])

Closing (dominant)

Cl.   39   antiphonal, 4 (1/1, 1/1) + 2-bar trans. (with dotted motive **y**)

DEVELOPMENT, bars 45–59

      45   reiteration of 2m trans., to series of *fp* desc. arps. (**b**)

      47   **b** in Dm; cir/5 prog. (prepared by dim. 7 on A): E♭m–B♭m–Fm–
            Cm–Gm–Dm–(each w/susps.)–N6/Dm with diss. 2nd and 7th
            – cad. on V/d (Germ. 6–V/d) to wind

      57   retrans. on turning figure (**z**), cir/5

RECAPITULATION, bars 60–101

First group (tonic)

1   60   **a** with 32nd-note answer in bass, imit. in treble (2 expanded to 2 + 2)

      64   **a** in bass to IV (2 + 1)

Br.   67   Bridge passage (remnant): secondary dev. on 32nds in vns,
            telescoped **a** motive in winds, *f-ff*, to martial rhythm

      73   **b** 2-bar frag., on V pedal; increasing wind solos

Second group (tonic)

2   76   same

Closing

Cl.   87   same, only 1-bar trans.

CODETTA

      92   **1a**, simply telescoping 2nd 2-bar unit

      99   3-bar ext., with repeated horn octaves (3 times as fast as horn
            octaves in Sym. 40/II)

Table 4.3. *"Jupiter" Symphony, III: Menuetto, Allegretto, C major, $\frac{3}{4}$, 59 bars; Trio, 28 bars*

MENUETTO

a	1	2-pt. texture, oscillating 2nd vn.
		m (4 + 4) + **n** (2 + 2, + 4) :‖
b	17	**m'** (2 + 2 + 4), + fanfare, elided with:
a'	28	**m** (4 + 4 + 4 + 4)
		m' (8, winds, chrom., imit.) + **n** (2 + 2, + 4) :‖

TRIO

c	1	**p** (cadence) + **q** (desc. fig.), 4 + 4 :‖
d	9	expansion of **p** (4 bars, cf. finale), 8 + 4 (retrans. on p)
c'	21	**p** + **q** :‖

Example 4.2.   Mozart, K. 551/II, themes and motives

Example 4.3.   Mozart, K. 551/III, Menuetto and Trio, opening phrases

Table 4.4. *"Jupiter" Symphony, IV: Molto allegro, C major, Alla breve, 423 bars*

EXPOSITION, bars 1–157:

First group (tonic)
1A bars 1–35, consisting of three musical ideas: (a) four whole notes, (x) sequel to a, beginning with repeated notes, (b) closing fanfare, itself consisting of a martial dotted motive in winds and brass and dotted-rhythm plus descending-scale figure in strings, in canon. Arranged as follows:

	1	a–x
	9	a–x'
	19	b
1B	36	fugal exposition on three-bar a to climactic statement (bar 53)

Bridge passage
| **Br.A** | 56 | c asc. scale motive (imit. and seq.) |
| **Br.B** | 64 | b fanfare in stretto |

Second group (dominant)
2A bars 74–94, consisting of a new theme with contrapuntal presence of previous motives:

| | 74 | d half-note theme, with descending eighths from b; imitation with c and d' (diminution of d) |
| 2B | 94 | stretto on d |

Closing (dominant)
| **Cl.A** | 115 | on x', with turn to C minor |
| **Cl.B** | 135 | on b (stretto and inversion), "Mannheim" cadence |

DEVELOPMENT, bars 158–224
	158	on a answered by b; G–E
	172	stretto imit. on b; cir/5: Am–D–G–C–F
	189³	on a answered by b; cir/5: Cm–Gm–Dm–[Am]–Em
	210	retrans. on b

RECAPITULATION, bars 225–356

First group (tonic)
1A	225	a + x
1B	233	a diss. seq. (beginning on c²–d²–e²–d²–c²) ***
Br.A	254	c imit., seq.
Br.B	262	b

Second group (tonic)
| 2A | 272 | d, with b, c, d' |
| 2B | 292 | stretto on d |

Closing (tonic)
| **Cl.A** | 313 | on x', with turn to F minor/D♭ major *** |
| **Cl.B** | 334 | on b (stretto and inversion), "Mannheim" cadence, to subdominant gesture |

Table 4.4 (*cont.*)

CODA, bars 357–423
    357   stretto on **a**
    371[2]   double fugue on **a** and **d** (=**1A** and **2A**); simultaneous canon on
              all motives but **x**; five-part invertible counterpoint ***
    402   closing on **x'** and **b**

Example 4.4.   Mozart, K. 551/IV, first theme

Table 4.5. *Permutation of counterpoint in "Jupiter"/IV, coda*

Source: Leonard Ratner, "*Ars combinatoria*: Chance and Choice in Eighteenth-
Century Music," in *Studies in Eighteenth-Century Music. A Tribute to Karl
Geiringer on His Seventieth Birthday*, ed. H. C. Robbins Landon with Roger
Chapman (New York, 1970), p. 361

Violin I			2	1	3	4	5	1
Violin II		2	1	3	4	5	2	3
Viola	2	1	3	4	5	2	1	2
Violoncello	1	3	4	5	2	1	3	4
Contrabass			2	1	3	4	5	

Example 4.5.   Mozart, K. 551/IV, coda, five-part counterpoint

5

Gesture and expectation: Allegro vivace

The first movement of the "Jupiter" has been variously described, in three books of the 1980s, as full of the "spirit of comic opera," as embodying a mixing of styles in "semiseria" fashion, and as being at once "monumental" and "saturated with the rhetoric that characterizes high comedy."[1] One key to understanding the multiplicity of expressive stances in this movement is the striking and persuasive idea of topics that has emerged from research into the period by Leonard Ratner and Wye J. Allanbrook: they argue that particular features of the music – rhythms, melodies, textures – represented familiar *topoi*, or topics, and that in this way Classical music was intelligible to its audience.[2] These topics included dance types, with their characteristic meters and gestures (for example, minuets, sarabandes), rhythms (sometimes connected with dance, as in the march, or in unrelated categories, like *alla zoppa*), and references to other styles and genres (recitative, aria, French overture, hunt, fanfare, pastoral, among many others).[3] Thus, the Classical composer may be seen as drawing on a common fund of musical types or "commonplaces," the source of ideas and arguments that constitutes *invention* (*inventio*), the first of the five parts of Classical rhetoric. Composers and audiences invested these commonplaces with meaning.

On the face of it, this is an attractive way to "decode" the language of the late eighteenth century. The principal problems concern the identification and limits of topics within a piece: what is a topic and what is not? Is every tremolo passage in a minor key a "reference" to *Sturm und Drang* or every imitative passage "learned style?"[4] Is a "fanfare" the same at the grand opening of the piece and in a calmer interior context? Does the composer intend the audience simply to recognize topics, or to understand more subtle meanings? The relevance of these concerns to the first movement of the "Jupiter" will be obvious in this chapter, which follows the tale of topics in three distinct thematic areas of the exposition: first group, second group, and closing group. Moreover, the topics chosen intersect with the high, middle, and low styles.

Example 5.1.   Haydn, Symphony No. 82/I ("The Bear")

In the broadest terms, the exposition charts a course from the grand style (first theme), down the stylistic spectrum to the singing style (second theme), then further down still to a comic, popular-style closing theme. The relationship between topical choice and dynamic level in articulating the form will be examined at the end of the chapter. Ultimately, the interplay of topics and dynamics will resonate in the Finale, to be discussed in Chapter 8; as a topical universe entire unto itself, the Allegro vivace nonetheless holds the keys to future events (see Table 4.1).

Topics and styles

The first theme begins with the sweeping gestures of the overtures to *Idomeneo* and *La clemenza di Tito*, and the slow introduction to the "Prague": martial *coups d'archet* (x), in Ratner's parlance,[5] reflecting the grand-style drama not only of the overture but of the Paris–Mannheim symphonic style which tended to begin with a big tutti passage in unison, often with repeated notes. (The Mannheim orchestra had relocated to Munich by the time of *Idomeneo*, and may have affected Mozart's elaborate symphonic style in that opera.) As Mozart had written to his father ten years earlier from Paris, he had been "careful not to neglect *le premier coup d'archet* [in his "Paris" Symphony, K. 297] – and that is quite sufficient. What a fuss the oxen here make of this trick! The devil take me if I can see any difference! They all begin together, just as they do in other places."[6] Haydn's celebrated symphony for Paris, No. 82 in C major ("The Bear"), similarly begins with a vigorous unison, in an arpeggiated tremolo (Example 5.1). And, just as in Mozart's earlier "Paris"

47

Symphony, K. 297 – which he was still having performed in Vienna in the mid-1780s – both Mozart and Haydn follow these big gestures with a softly lyrical harmonized counterstatement (y).[7] Haydn's sequel strikingly changes the topic, to minuet (bar 3), then returns to a tutti fanfare (z) to bring the first group to a stirring half cadence; the opening idea is then recast, *piano* and with a counterfigure, ultimately leading to the modulatory transition. Mozart's sequel in the "Jupiter," called "singing style" by Ratner, is actually a gentler kind of march, making explicit the intrada-like dotted rhythm implied by the opening upbeat flourishes. After a symmetrical restatement (V–I), again alternating *forte* and *piano*, the big tutti returns, now with a definite fanfare-like march rhythm (♩ ♩. ♪ ♩ ♩) and the sweeping ascending flourishes, now going in both directions.

The "grand style" thus encompasses complementary topics (x + y). And while contrasts in dynamics and articulation heighten surface distinctions among these topics, their rhythmic gestures are closely related. This is made clear in the next section, 1b, which, like the Haydn "Bear," begins with a soft version of the opening. Moreover, the *forte–piano* opposition of the opening two motives is now resolved in two entirely different ways. First, the soft restatement has an octave-span counterfigure (w) in the winds that unites the registers of the x and y motives, mediated by the horns; the counterfigure is the same as a prominent main-theme motive in the "Prague" Symphony (I, bars 43–5). And second, dynamic opposition is played out over a much longer time-span: first, both motives are subsumed into a *piano* section without bass instruments (bars 24–36), then a longer *forte* tutti beginning on the dominant and ending in a half-cadence in that key (bars 37–55). Thus, the shorter dynamically-contrasted segments of the first group (8 [2+2, 2+2] + 15) give way to the bigger blocks of *piano* and *forte* (13 + 19) in the modulatory section (1b–Br.).

The second theme (2a), a charmingly balanced singing-style period with wind accents (m + m + n), is notable for several reasons. Its initial texture – first-violin melody and oscillating second-violin accompaniment – recurs at the beginning of the Menuet and the beginning of the Finale, as noted in Chapter 4. Second, the pseudo-imitation of the first three notes by the bass forecasts that texture during recurrences of the four-note theme of the Finale, as well as pointing up the bass register as the site of the first fragmented appearance of the y motive (bar 71), leading to the closing phrases of the second theme. Mozart's second themes not infrequently have a kind of tripartite structure (a–a'–b), in which the last is a cadential phrase; the lengthier "Prague" second theme has just this structure. Finally, rather than closing, or introducing a closing section, the theme trails off in a figure of doubt or questioning (*dubitatio* [*Zweifel*] or *interrogatio* [*Frage*])[8] a series of ascending chords ending in a five-beat grand pause, rare in Mozart at such a place. A "shock" effect answers this question, a disruptive C-minor tutti chord with emphatic timpani (2b, bars 81–2) inaugurating what appears to be a closing section on a diminution of y (2c, bar 88). While the ultimate effect of this C-minor chord will not become known until the Finale, its purpose here is to reassert the grand style with the rhetorical force of direct address, combining the emotionally powerful figures of *aposiopesis* (breaking off) and *apostrophe* (turning to another topic for effect).[9] Mozart, to use the authoritarian metaphor common in music criticism, forces his audience to make a swerve into a startling new region. Every previous and subsequent pause is at a cadence and ushers in a melodic theme, as does the diminished-y passage to come (bar 100).

Another radical shift in style is heralded by the reassuringly folk-like plucked notes of bass and viola together with a broken-chord accompaniment before the melody begins (bar 101). This melody, the "true" closing theme, asserts the popular style of comic theater, a highly repetitive aria melody, while recasting the dotted rhythm of y as a newly light-hearted "tail" pattern, z^1 followed by z^2 (bars 107–8). Only at the very end of the exposition is the emphatic grand style of the opening theme recalled. Charles Rosen has suggested that square-cut, popular-style melodies are not infrequently found in the closing section because they "ground the tension previously generated" in a show of "cadential force."[10] But the importation of an actual aria segment (from "Un bacio di mano," K. 541) invites speculation. The text of the inserted passage is "Voi siete un po' tondo, mio car Pompeo,/L'usanze del mondo andate a studiar" ("You are a bit innocent, my dear Pompeo,/Go study the ways of the world"). Is it too far-fetched to suggest that the prominence of this closing theme in the development section owes something to the text's admonition to gain experience? The winds first hand it over into the quasi-deception of E♭ major (in a descending gesture similar to that in the G-minor Symphony and adapted by Beethoven in his First Symphony), and in subsequent fragmentations it loses its geniality together with its pizzicato and *piano* as triple-stopped chords, the march rhythm, and minor keys (F minor, G minor, D minor, and A minor) come to the fore in *forte* (bars 133–53). And this first section of the development remains tonally confused even within the narrow range of its keys because it keeps moving sequentially over the same territory while the size of the unit (subphrase) and the time-interval of imitation keep changing:

bar 133: asc. seq. on z^2: 2-bar unit, imit. at 1-bar interval   E♭–Fm–Gm
bar 139: desc. seq. on z^2: 2-bar unit, imit. at 1/2-bar int. (stretto)   Gm–Fm–E♭
bar 143: desc. seq. on z^2: 4-bar unit, imit. at 1/2-bar int. (stretto)   E♭–Cm–Gm
bar 147: seq. on z^1 and z^2: 2m., then 1 bar unit, alternating   Gm–Dm–Am

Compare this progression with the very regular one in the development of the G-minor Symphony (four-measure sequences finally decreasing to two measures, in bars 104–7, 108–11, 112–15; 115–18, 119–22, 123–6, 127–30; 131–2, 133–4, 135–6, 137–8) and especially the logical decrease in the size of the sequential unit in the development of the "Prague" Symphony, which even the complicated motivic texture of that piece cannot dislodge:

bar 143:   8 (6+2) + 5 (4+1)
bar 156:   6 (2+2+2)
bar 162:   4 (2+2) + 4 (2+2) + 2
bar 172:   2 (1+1) + 2 (1+1) + 1

Part of what makes the "Jupiter" development section unable to settle on a sustained pattern of sequences and imitations is its clash of topics and the styles of which they are a part: the appearance of march and minor had in the exposition been associated only with the grand style, and so the confusion here is generated by what may be termed topical dissonance. An ostensibly clear retransition passage on V of vi (A minor) offers a way out, returning to *piano*, and featuring the directional descent that characterizes many of Mozart's preparations for the recapitulation, notably those in the "Prague" and G-minor Symphonies.[11] But this preparation turns out to be a red herring, for it leads to a return of the main theme in the subdominant, F major. And while some sonata-form movements actually do begin their recapitulations in the subdominant (notably the beginners' Sonata in C major, K. 545, first movement, and the Quartet in G major, K. 387, Finale), in the "Jupiter" the return of the opening theme in IV quickly calls attention to its status as an interlude in the development. Is this a so-called "false recapitulation"?

"False recapitulations," "false retransitions," and the "reprise-interlude"

The meaning of the common term "false recapitulation" is not self-evident, as the lack of scholarly consensus attests. Writers agree that it involves the reprise of the main theme, at some point during the development section, but the principal area of controversy is the key in which that theme appears. I will leave out of account a technique common in the 1760s and 1770s, called "premature reprise" by Oliver Strunk and "precursory recapitulation" by Mark Evan Bonds, in which the theme is stated sequentially at the beginning of the development, first in the dominant, then in the tonic, before further development; this technique is not relevant to Mozart's late symphonies, even if theorists like Koch still described it in the 1790s.[12] Bonds believes only false recapitulations in the tonic can be considered as such; Charles Rosen extends this to the subdominant as well, asserting that "if a reprise is not in the tonic (or the subdominant), it fools only the uneducated."[13] James Webster allows false recapitulations in other keys, giving as an example Haydn's Symphony No. 102, a movement in B♭ major with a return to the main theme in C major.[14] Janet Levy takes it for granted not only that false recapitulations occur in the wrong key, listing Haydn's No. 102 and the "Jupiter" as examples, but that the composer intends the listener *not* to be fooled.[15] In the main, discussion of the technique centers on Haydn, its principal practitioner in the realm of tonic returns. Mozart tended not to write such self-consciously formal articulations in the tonic. The real questions are these: what defining features ought a false recapitulation to have? Should off-tonic returns of the main theme be included? And, critically, is the purpose of the first theme "return" in the development (whatever we may call it) always to mislead the listener into thinking that it really is the recapitulation or may the purpose sometimes be something different?

Let us grant, as Bonds would have us do, that "false recapitulation" ought to be reserved for prepared returns of the main theme in the tonic during the development section. What then is the status of the subdominant main-theme return in the "Jupiter"? I would argue that there are three types of *off-tonic* appearances of the main theme in sonata-form development sections. The first one, not really at issue here, uses the main theme and its motives as subject for development, as is standard practice in innumerable works (for example, the first movement of the G-minor, K. 550, where the main theme is immediately treated in sequence and then polyphonically recombined). The second type is a reasonably complete thematic statement, possibly given a little preparation, that in scoring resembles the opening, and that often diverges harmonically or in phrase structure after a single period. Falling into this category is the subdominant return in the overture to *Don Giovanni*. I call this a "reprise-interlude" because of its temporary sense of arrival and its relaxation of tension, what Rosen calls "a brief moment of consonance in the most dissonant section of the work."[16]

Finally, there is the "Jupiter" prototype, which requires a preparatory passage that mimics the gestures of a true retransition, followed by an off-tonic statement of the main theme that *immediately* announces itself as suspiciously unlike what a real recapitulation would be. Not only does the quiet version with countermelody appear, rather than the tutti beginning, but the prominence of the bassoons in playing that countermelody radically disconfirms the moment as recapitulatory. Thus, what is critical here is that a recapitulation is *expected*, not that the listener is momentarily misled when it appears. Expectation is produced by the thinning out of orchestral texture – the alternation of strings and winds in bars 153–7 – and by the downward pull of bars 157–60. Janet Levy points to such thinning as evidence of preparation for a new beginning; indeed, retransitions in Haydn and Mozart symphonies use this device with striking frequency.[17] What is false here – what misleads the listener – is really the retransition, since there is palpably no recapitulation. Following the "false retransition," then, is a *false* "reprise-interlude," false compared to the *Don Giovanni* overture not because it sounds like a recapitulation but because we were expecting one. Temporarily returning to a spacious presentation of part of the first theme is not enough; the role of preparation is critical. In this context, it is important to note that the passage following the interlude, a tense and furious series of x flourishes over a descending chromatic bass line,[18] begins in A minor (bar 171), the key initially prepared by the false retransition; in retrospect, the reprise-interlude may be seen less as a point of arrival and more as a deceptive interpolation (Example 5.2):

	false retr.	rep.-int.				
key	E	F	C	D	E	Am
Am:	V	vi	V/vi seq.	(V/g) seq.	V	i
bar	155	161	165	167	169	171

In the development section of the "Jupiter," then, the clash of topics plotted by the main theme and closing theme of the exposition is resolved not in the head-to-head combat of simultaneous development, but in the consecutively stated false retransition and reprise-interlude that subsume both. We might

Example 5.2.   Mozart, K. 551/I, bars 157–71: harmonic structure

consider the false retransition and recapitulation-interlude to be "formal" topics – topics of interior reference – rather than exterior topics, such as those derived from the dance.

The role of dynamics in articulating sonata form

In a symphony, dynamic contrast is often a result of such obvious factors as the antiphonal opposition of strings or winds (*piano*) versus tutti (*forte*), or a vigorous opening versus a gentler theme strategically placed in a less exposed position. However, in sonata form movements, different functional areas are often delineated from one another by the same strategic means, lending to dynamic and textural change a status as formal identifier.

Theorists of the later eighteenth century – among others, Riepel, Vogler, Koch, and Daube – often discussed different areas in sonata form in terms of general qualities, such as "rushing," "sonorous," "brilliant," on the one hand, and "singing," "gentle," "melodious," on the other. What is not clear is the extent to which these designations match our views, inherited from nineteenth-century descriptions of form, of a "first-theme type" and a "second-theme type," respectively. Indeed, Jane Stevens has concluded from a study of writings by Vogler and others that the contrasts described may be nothing more than the *forte–piano* openings of pieces like the "Jupiter," rather than a ratification of contrasting character and dynamics in first and second themes.[19] Koch, on the other hand, probably did mean his "singing phrase" to refer to the theme after a definite cadence in the dominant.[20]

Mozart's last four symphonies quite strikingly exploit the massed blocks of *piano* strings versus *forte* tutti that Haydn favored in such pieces as Symphony No. 88 (1787). If we examine the dynamic levels of the first-movement expositions, we find that every functional area of the exposition, and by consequence the recapitulation, has a distinct dynamic profile. The simplest is No. 39, after the slow introduction: first group (1) is *p*, bridge (Br.) is *f*, second group (2) is *p*, closing (Cl.) is *f*, with the alternation continuing in the development section. As is typical, the retransition is soft. Slightly more complex are Nos. 38 and 40, which subdivide the functional areas. In the G minor, the order is:

1: *p f* (a fanfare)
Br.: *p f*
2: *p* cresc
Cl.: *f p f*

with the alternation continuing in the development. In the "Prague," on the other hand, the main theme is more complex, dynamically and motivically:

1a: $p\,f\,p$
1b: f
Br.: $p\,f$
2: p
Cl.(=1b): f

The "Linz," No. 36, alternates dynamics in every area but the bridge.

Finally, the "Jupiter" is the most dynamically complex in the first group, but contains a regular alternation in the other areas:

1: $f\,p\,f\,p\,f$
Br.: $p\,f$
2: $p\,f$
Cl.: $p\,f$

Moreover, nearly every one of these dynamic changes is articulated either with a pause or a big cadence, and in both the secondary and closing groups the *piano* segment introduces a new theme. The resemblance to Haydn's Symphony No. 88 is significant, because it points up characteristic features of each composer's style. Every one of No. 88's functional areas begins with a variant of the main theme (eighth notes), each continues with another version of that theme accompanied by sixteenth notes, and with the exception of the bridge, which is all *forte*, note values and dynamics are correlated: every area moves from *piano* eighths to *forte* sixteenths. As I have argued elsewhere, this exemplifies Haydn's paratactic (repetition-based) sonata-form construction as well as his interest in single-theme explorations.[21] The "Jupiter," on the other hand, highlights both second group and closing area with new themes, the latter of these particularly extravagant because a closing passage had already been introduced after the C-minor "shock" (2b). Mozart sought contrast in discrete thematic units, as the pauses between sections attest, but rationalized them with Haydn's dynamic blocking.

6

Structure and expression: *Andante cantabile*

The Andante cantabile of the "Jupiter" is a kind of distillation of its companions in the symphonies of 1788 and in the "Prague," since it is considerably shorter yet no less powerful.[1] Indeed, whereas the outer movements of these works are remarkably distinct from each other in musical personality, the slow movements all disrupt their lyrical flow with disturbing transitional passages of powerful emotional expressiveness. We simply do not see this in earlier symphony Andantes by Mozart. But we have seen it in some of the piano concertos of Mozart's glory years in Vienna, 1784–6, and the suggestion may be advanced that those concertos deepened his later symphonic slow movements just as they transformed his orchestration.[2] I will refer to the works by their numbers here so as not to create confusion in keys (for example, the slow movement of the G minor is in E♭ major, the key of a different symphony).

"Expressive episodes"

In Mozart's last four symphonies, the Andantes initially induce a reverie in the beautiful sound-world of their principal themes, only to shatter it with varying degrees of force in a suddenly *forte* transitional passage. All but No. 40 turn to minor at that point, and all within a few bars move toward (or farther around) the flat side of the circle of fifths, which gives emphasis and poignancy to the stirring rhythms, syncopations, offbeat accents, and other signals of heightened affect. Initially appearing simply to modulate to the dominant at the bridge, No. 40 more insidiously removes the main theme to a remote region of mysterious beauty, on a Baroque circle-of-fifths progression beginning in D♭ major, filled with suspensions – after which it can never again be interpreted the same way. This older-style progression was standard practice for composers two and three generations before Mozart but is hardly ever found in works by his contemporaries; it accounts, I believe, for some of the most moving moments in his music. Indeed, Mozart often must use violent means to return to the main thread of his discourse after such a stylistic digression: witness the dissonance in bar 33 of Symphony No. 40 and bar 55 of No. 41 (to be discussed below).

In charting a path to understanding the Andante of No. 39 in the terms of musical experience as described around 1800, Leo Treitler singles out such words as "narrative," "poetry," "fantasy," "the enigmatic," and "discourse" in writings of Wackenroder, Tieck, Schlegel, Körner, and Novalis.[3] His imaginative reading of the movement hinges on the distinction between (and intersection of) musical convention ("the underlying patterns of conventional genres and implicit constraints arising from the grammar of style") and narrative convention ("the progressive interpretation of these determinants through the unfolding of the work in time") and uncovers a wealth of detail, sharply observed. He is especially vital on the disruptive passages (bars 30–8, 46–9):

The innocent cadential figure leaps over the double bar into the relative minor, its repeated eighth-notes drawn out to a full measure, with the shrill coloration of woodwinds (especially so when played on eighteenth-century instruments!) . . . this device unleashes an outburst: a wide melodic range traversed back and forth in angry pacing, a heavily dissonant sonority, strong thrusts in the harmonic motion, a highly agitated rhythmic surface, shrillness of orchestral color. The passage has the character of desperate thinking, looking for a way out, first in one direction, then in another.[4]

Interestingly, the stable passage in the dominant attained after all the turmoil (bar 54) is strikingly similar both to the main theme of No. 40's slow movement in its imitative building-up of a pattern of repeated notes with suspensions and to the second theme in the slow movement of Mozart's "Dissonant" Quartet, K. 465.[5] But the "desperate thinking" of the passage in No. 39 described by Treitler is not echoed in the searing bridge passage of No. 41; Treitler's imagery helps us articulate the differences between them.

In the slow movement of the "Jupiter" the small ideas that resonate with its predecessors have large expressive consequences. No. 40 recasts its opening theme with the parts inverted (bar 9), so that the imitative repeated notes are in the bass, an augmented version of the bass line now in the treble. No. 41 makes a double exchange: first the melody goes into the bass (bar 11) with an ornate countermelody; then at the recapitulation (bar 60) treble and bass constantly switch roles, with theme and figuration appearing in each register. Indeed, it is the activation of the bass register that engulfs and subverts the main-theme return at bar 60. But where else in the symphonies do we find such detailed, slurred thirty-second-note figuration? Passagework in No. 39

is largely dotted and hence related to the first theme; in the "Prague" there are some lushly chromatic sixteenth-note passages; the "Haffner" contains figurations in thirty-seconds but these are articulated with slurs and dots and set in the middle strings as thematic material. In fact, the only orchestral pieces from this period with any detailed figuration in the slow movements are the piano concertos, and even there it is neither a routine nor an extensive occurrence. By contrast, Haydn's symphonies of the 1780s have much more extensive figuration in the slow movements, especially Nos. 76 (Adagio ma non troppo), 77 (Andante sostenuto), and 79 (Adagio cantabile). Haydn also wrote Adagios much more often than Mozart, who once noted in a letter: "Please tell my sister that there is no adagio in any of these concertos [the first four of 1784] – only andantes."[6]

The answer to the figuration question lies in the designation "cantabile" for this movement, which is used by Mozart in no other symphonic slow movement. Immediately striking is the unaccompanied muted violin in the first bar, singing out a sarabande rhythm. This single line, even though joined after only two beats, heralds an improvisatory quality rarely found in Mozart's symphonies but more characteristic of Haydn; indeed, the leisurely pace is established at the outset when the consequent phrase, begun by both violins, embellishes the first bar, then expands the expected final two bars (what would be a II^6–I_4^6–V–I cadence at bars 7–8) into five. The expansion is a cadence in slow motion: a full bar of IV (bar 7), a full bar of I_4^6 (bar 8), and then a re-traversal of the same harmonic territory just covered in bars 6–8 (now at bars 9–10). By contrast, the second set of matched phrases is just that (bars 11–14, 15–18), and offers the orchestral layering effect of the piano concertos: melody in lower strings, pulsating eighth-note chords in horns and bassoons, and graceful figuration in the violins. While elisions and expansions of phrases are basic elements of late eighteenth-century musical style, it is still unusual to find them so early in a piece.

Each of the elements thus far recounted, all in the first eighteen bars – the "personal" figurations, the layering, and the elided, expanded phrase – will be recast in contexts that might be termed "hyperexpressive," that generate the dark-hued coloration of so much of the Andante. In bar 19, Mozart radically changes the rhetoric of the movement with a sudden outburst in C minor, reminiscent of the shocking C-minor tutti chord in the first movement at bar 81 (2b). Also charging the moment is the constant stress on the pitch C, in the bass for the first four bars, in the violin for the next four. Finally, this passage conflates and intensifies three of the most powerful ideas in Symphonies Nos. 39 and 40: the sustained winds of No. 39 during the passage

Example 6.1.   Mozart, K. 551/II, development:
bars 51–6, rebarred harmonic reduction

of wild alarm described above, bars 31ff. (Treitler called them "shrill"), the quick two-note figure of No. 40, bars 29ff., now an agitated appoggiatura in sixteenth-triplets, and the dissonant ascending chromatic line of No. 40, bars 44–6. The last of these is made almost unbearably intense by the shortened and thus more frequent descending arpeggios from c^3 in the first violin (every two beats), resulting in a syncopated pattern both at the level of the sixteenth note and in a temporary perception of rebarring of the triple meter into four duple and one quadruple bars (23–6). The reiterated Cs and the rising chromatic line inevitably raise the spectre of the Statue scene in the Act II Finale of *Don Giovanni*.[7]

Virtually the entire development section is occupied by this material, beginning and ending in D minor (a key already alluded to in bars 6, 9, 32, and 35) and thus suggesting the middle section of an ABA movement rather more than a sonata development; in Haydn's hands the B section is often just such a fierce outbreak. Now in the "duple" passage (bars 51–5, Example 6.1, rebarred) even the violin ascends, in a Baroque-style circle-of-fifths passage starting on E♭ minor (around the circle to V/D minor) that is less dissonant than in the exposition, yet with each fresh ascent the suspensions seem more sharply pointed, creating ever greater yearning. Is it literally the past that the music tries so desperately to embrace? Once again, the only way we can be jolted back to awareness of the themes and world at hand is by a wrenching dissonance, the Neapolitan sixth of D minor (E♭ major) with painfully suspended As and Fs. Evocations of an older style in Mozart do not merely recall Vivaldi or Corelli; they serve rather to open up a distant, elevated vista whose effect transcends anything like "stylistic influence" or "historical intertextuality" and instead conjures with the rhetorical sublime. Certainly *imitatio* was a central part of rhetorical teaching, and, were one to emulate the most sublime authors of the past, sublimity might be the result in the present.

Mozart invoked this realm of historical harmonies often in minor circle-of-fifths- or subdominant-oriented passages, especially those with suspensions. While it is unsurprising to find such a passage in church music, such as the incomparable *Jesu Christe* of the Mass in C minor, K. 427, with its simple yet breathtaking plunge into a chain of suspended chords (C: I–IV⁶–IV/IV–IV–V–I–V/V–V), Mozart, far more often than his contemporaries and certainly more often than Haydn, brought these progressions into his instrumental compositions where they show the power of an elevated style beyond the grand gesture.[8]

Genre, topic, and "secondary development"

Two other major works of the period used a sarabande topic: the Andante of the G-major Piano Concerto, K. 453 (1784) and the "Dissonant" Quartet in C major, K. 465 (January 1785); the latter, like the "Jupiter," has an F-major Andante cantabile.[9] The sarabande may be described as a "slow minuet" whose characteristic feature is an emphasis on the second beat in triple meter (| ♩ ♩. ♪ |), lending it a "deliberate, serious character which represented the high style."[10] Both the Concerto and Quartet have a more hymn-like rhythm than the Symphony, at least at the outset; and the Quartet, because it is in "slow-movement sonata form" with "secondary development" (that is, a sonata form in which development is displaced to the recapitulation, and only a retransition separates exposition and recapitulation),[11] bears a closer structural resemblance to the F-major Andante of the C-major Quintet, K. 515 (1787), than to either of the orchestral works. The Quartet's bridge passage maintains an eighth-note pulsation in the inner voices with suspensions, and finally creates the same rebarring effect as in the "Jupiter": from bars 20–2 there are four duple units. As if to complicate the resemblances, the second theme of the Quartet (bars 26ff.) builds up its repeated-note motive imitatively and with suspensions just like the second theme of No. 39, while the rhythmic pattern of those repeated notes (| ♩ ♪♪♪♪ |), reiterated chordally at the close, is identical to the main theme of the Quintet's Andante. As in No. 41, the most affectively heightened portion of the Quartet is the expanded bridge passage, although the difference in structure means the placement of the Symphony's passage in the development occurs earlier than that of the Quartet's passage in the recapitulation.

The bridge also creates a telling similarity between Concerto and Symphony. As we have seen, the Symphony enters the despairing world of the bridge rather suddenly, with only a triadic wind upbeat to change direction, and its

Example 6.2.   Mozart, Piano Concerto in G major, K. 453/II

downbeat-heavy rhythms (the rest are syncopated) overcome the second-beat orientation of the sarabande. The Concerto Andante opens with a profound "motto" phrase, an open question ending with a fermata on the rest after the dominant (Example 6.2). Throughout the movement, the sequel to this motto is contested ground, never returning to the lyrical oboe melody that supplants it in the opening ritornello. It is heard four more times: (1) at the beginning of the solo exposition (bar 30), followed by a sudden thick G-minor chord (the minor dominant, just as in K. 551); (2) at the beginning of the development, played by the tutti (bar 64), followed by a sorrowing solo melody in D minor; (3) at the beginning of the recapitulation (bar 90), played by the soloist and followed by a thick E♭-major chord (for the first time retaining the sarabande rhythm); and (4) in the coda (bar 123), where the winds (the only group not yet to have played it) give it a little spin into the subdominant instead of the unanswerable fermata, and the piano is finally able to answer and resolve it, as a sarabande.[12] This suggests that the reason it could not be answered before is that it was asking the wrong question.

The first theme in the "Jupiter" is also contested ground: it is never allowed to end. Mozart achieves this by interrupting it in its first appearance and then making it yield to figuration. In the recapitulation, however, he creates a much bigger disruption by bringing in a secondary development which, in a slow movement with an emotionally intense development section, is structurally unnecessary and expressively redundant. Yet Mozart found in this secondary development a brutally effective way to neutralize the previous topics and still the unquiet bridge. First the *a* theme is overtaken by figuration (bar 62), then completely replaced by a rhythmic development in the winds (bars 67–72). Its dotted rhythm remains, but thoroughly transformed in affect until, in pure martial C major, it is emptied of all reference to the movement (Example 6.3).[13] In this critical moment, bars 71–2, the *fortissimo* march fanfare negates the sarabande as it absorbs the bridge, which is now reduced to two bars of vestigial uneasiness (bars 73–4). Even in the

Example 6.3.   Mozart, K. 551/II, "secondary development"

coda, the first theme cannot shake off an interruption, in the bars Mozart added as an afterthought.

Opposing these highly personal visions is a broadly affirmative tutti theme in both Concerto and Symphony: in K. 453 it appears only in the ritornello (bar 19) and recapitulation (bar 111), and in K. 551 it is the second theme, where it can expand. It has the same harmonic structure as the first theme (I–V–V–I) in its first phrase, while the sequel is a sequence of dominant sevenths set to a descending chromatic line in the winds, nicely offsetting the ascending line of the bridge. In addition, the sequel tames earlier figuration completely: sequence, imitation, and correlation with the accompaniment pattern. As in the first theme, however, the cadence is extended deceptively toward the subdominant side; marked with a crescendo, it returns to the thick scoring of the bridge, and to something of the same questing quality.

All of the disturbing elements of this movement – the changing nature of the figuration, the themes that are overtaken by forces outside themselves, the distant sublime of the bridge in exposition and development, the martial climax that occupies the bridge in the recapitulation – have perhaps been stressed at the expense of its more balanced aspects. I have chosen to read the expansion of the first theme, beginning in bar 7, as a derailment, when in fact it could be seen as a broadening, in tone color as well as in phrase structure, of its structural and expressive potential. Indeed, subsequent events show there is no place in the movement for as thinly textured and pensive an opening theme as *a* was originally. When the theme comes back at the very end (introduced by the same kind of retransitional line that had ended the exposition), it is allowed two unaccompanied beats, but then wind figuration returns. It is possible that Mozart had to mediate between the sarabande topic and the expressive language of the symphony. But he also had available the resources of the "secondary development" in slow-movement form, which he used here to resituate the sarabande as simply too delicate for the massed orchestral force needed to make a glimpse of the past sublime.

7

Phrase rhythm: Menuetto, Allegretto

At a time when composers did not challenge the two-reprise structure and inevitable double bars of the minuet and trio, the stereotyped metric and rhythmic characteristics of these movements became an inviting target for originality and wit. Haydn at the end of his life may have wished for someone to write "a really *new* Minuet," but no exhaustion of possibilities is evident in either his or Mozart's symphonies.[1] Two significant features of the Menuetto and Trio movement will form the principal subject of this chapter: the intricate relationship between phrase rhythm, dynamics, and orchestration that characterizes the Menuetto, and the often-remarked final cadence that begins the Trio. In 1976, Leonard B. Meyer devoted nearly seventy pages to an explication of the Trio of Mozart's G-minor Symphony, K. 550.[2] The length of the study vindicated his premise, that his earlier assertion that "complexity was at least a necessary condition for value" in music was "if not entirely mistaken, at least somewhat confused," because "what is crucial is relational richness, and such richness (or complexity) is in no way incompatible with simplicity of musical vocabulary and grammar."[3] Indeed, he suggests that the listener is able to appreciate the complexities of the Trio "precisely *because* these arise out of uncomplicated, unassuming tonal means" (emphasis added).[4] In this chapter, the tension between simplicity and complexity will form the background of the discussion.

Menuetto

The beginning of the Menuetto is unstable. In a thin texture played only by the violins for two bars, the piece lacks a tonic pitch until bar 2, a bass register until bar 3, and most strikingly, a strong downbeat or sense of meter. Most of Mozart's minuets begin *forte*; this one not only begins *piano*, but its wavering accompaniment and slurred melody trace a descent that withholds arrival.[5] The third bar is that point of arrival, articulated not only by melody and bass on the tonic pitch, but by the festive punctuation of horns (supporting the melody) and clarini and timpani (supporting the bass). The reiteration of this pattern in bars 4–8 appears to confirm not only the presence of hyperbars of two bars in length, but also a "reversed" metric and dynamic accentuation, with the structural downbeat occurring in the second unit. Thus, Mozart appears deliberately to contravene the various kinds of *pas de menuet*, all of which had a basic unit of two bars in length, so that "while the dancer's movements always imply an accent on the first beat of a unit, strong secondary accents would not necessarily fall on the second downbeat."[6]

But then Mozart abandons the pattern he initiated, and proceeds on a course of decreasing the size of the unit while speeding up its rhythmic articulations. He also separates the bass elements into timpani and contrabass.[7] The new *forte* two-bar incise (Koch's term for a sub-phrase)[8] is repeated literally (bars 9–10, 11–12), and each time has a drum stroke on its first downbeat (the first of every two bars), while having the contrabass support the downbeat in every bar. In the final four-bar phrase (13–16) timpani play on nearly every downbeat (13, 14, 16) in addition to the bass on every beat until the cadence. Thus, in the first reprise, the basses and timpani do not always coordinate with

Table 7.1. *Metric organization of Menuetto, first reprise*

Phrase structure

bars 1–8	*p*	2 + 2	2 + 2
bars 9–12	*f*	2 — 1 + 1	2 — 1 + 1
bars 13–16	*f*	1 1 1 1	:‖:

Articulation of downbeats

timp		>	>			>	>	
bars 1–8	|	|	|	|		|	|	|	|
bass		>	>			>	>	
timp	>		>					
bars 9–12	|	|	|	|				
bass	>	>	>	>				
timp	>	>		>				
bars 13–16	|	|	|	|				
bass	>>>	>>>	>>>	>				

the strings, and the heavy stresses they provide articulate first hyperbars, then bars, then individual beats. At the same time, the melody starts on a higher pitch in every four-bar unit (in the last unit, the highest pitch is in the second bar, 14), creating a different model of intensification. Table 7.1 shows this structure.

Two surprising turns in the second period vividly demonstrate the elasticity of Mozart's manipulation of phrases. Beginning with a typical dominant-pedal reiteration of the opening rhythmic patterns (b), the story of the second period changes with the two fanfare echoes (bars 24–6 and 26–8) at the end of the dominant-pedal passage (see Table 4.3). They run headlong into what starts out as the return to the main melody at bar 28: the collision turned into an elision, so to speak. The source of the fanfare is the dominant pedal itself, using the rhythmic pattern of the last phrase in the first reprise (13–16) to make the head bite the tail at the appropriate spot (28). But instead of a literal return, the rising pitch level of each phrase in a generates an explicit connection between them in a': the second half of each four-bar phrase simply moves back up the scale to the next higher starting place, each one now temporarily tonicized instead of acting like a consequent. Brass and timpani or brass alone emphasize the second hyperbar in each phrase (30–1, 34–5, 38–9), thus maintaining the weak–strong accentuation of the opening phrase. Thus we have exactly the same number of bars as in the first reprise, ending with a full cadence on C major in bar 43.

In bar 44 is the second surprising turn: a densely chromatic imitative wind passage precisely eight bars long, followed by the transposition of the second eight bars of the first reprise, complete with an expanded role for the timpani. Consider the effect of these two passages: first, they confirm that the full cadence in bar 43 was not grounded enough to end the minuet, because of the transformation of the pseudo-return into a big sequence (28–31, 32–5, 36–9) with only four bars of closing (40–3). Second, the soft linear wind passage stands in the same relation to the *forte* tutti passage as did the first two bars of the minuet to the second two bars: soft linear strings to tonic arrival articulated by bass and timpani. Suddenly the hyperbar has grown to eight bars, which may be why the timpani work overtime to cut the last eight bars down to manageable proportions. Thus, after the dominant-pedal and fanfare passage, Mozart presents two sixteen-bar sections (28–43, 44–50) each ending in the tonic, each beginning with the melody of a in the same register but confounding the sense of return by means of excessive repetition, sequential in the first case and imitative in the second.

We might ask – why go to all this trouble to avoid a more standard return?

Table 7.2. *Points of melodic descent in K. 551/III, Menuetto*

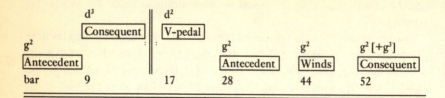

The answer is the pitch on which the final eight bars begin – g^2 – as well as the consequent melody. The melody in bars 52–9 is virtually identical (in initial pitches and in contour) to the melody in bars 1–8 (Table 7.2). The elaborate deflecting and reorchestrating manages to defamiliarize precisely that opening series of descending half-steps from g^2. The irony here is that Mozart defamiliarizes those pitches by keeping them in plain view.

Trio

The Trio has attracted analysts because of its simple inversion of a conventional device: the piece opens with a final cadence. Ratner goes so far as to suggest that because the cadence figure is used for everything *but* a final cadence, the whole purpose of the trio is "to put the cadence out of countenance."[9] The cadence does several things not hitherto mentioned. In beginning with a heavy downbeat, it inverts the stress-pattern of the minuet, which began with a two-bar upbeat. It resolves, in register and instrumentation, the chromatic wind passage in the minuet, in which the leading tone in bar 51 never went to the tonic. It prepares the A-minor passage after the double bar, notable for foreshadowing the four-note subject of the Finale. It creates a virtual parody of dance movements in the oom-pah-pah passage with the melody notes slurred (bars 17–20) which serves at once as retransition – the winds bring in the cadence figure in the tonic as part of the sequence but suddenly static in rhythm – and motivic development of the cadence.

Finally, I believe that it injects an overt rhetorical figure into the proceedings, but one quite different from the pieces in which Haydn began with a final cadence: the G-major Quartet, Op. 33 No. 5, first movement, or Symphony No. 57, slow movement. Haydn actually used the same cadence-pattern as an ending as well as an opening, to create the framing device of the figure *epanalepsis*. While there are several rhetorical figures for simply altering the expected word-order, I find most appropriate the daunting term *hysteron-proteron* to describe Mozart's inverted ending–beginning order: "the stylistic decision to put the cart before the horse in order to make him push it."[10] This attractive image exemplifies precisely what it is about this final cadence that has been so unusual all along: it is literally "like a cart," that is, it has no power to move by itself, because patently it is unlike the vast majority of actual final cadences of trios or minuets. Were the first two bars more appropriately at the end of a reprise, the entire penultimate bar would consist of a single chord in all voices, forcing to a stop the momentum of the graceful or vigorous dance. Only in the lengthy trio of the G-major Quartet, K. 387, is there such a final cadence, where it has been prepared in each section by a passage with slowly-moving chords (one per bar) in the lower strings while the first violin hovers around a single note.[11] Thus, to identify the opening as a final cadence makes necessary the question "of what is it the final cadence?" Certainly not of the phrase that follows it.

8

The rhetoric of the learned style: Finale, Molto allegro

Even had Mozart known in advance that this would be the last movement of his last symphony, he could not have surpassed the "Jupiter" finale. A pithy summary of his achievement has proved elusive, however. The simple description of the movement as a synthesis of sonata form and fugue, or, as Einstein put it, of "galant" and "learned" styles, fails to suggest an innovation beyond that of the Quartet in G major, K. 387, or the C-major Symphony by Michael Haydn completed not quite six months before the "Jupiter."[1] In this chapter, I offer an interpretation of the "Jupiter" finale that revises the terms of discussing the learned style. As we have seen in Chapter 2, the persistence of such stylistic dichotomies and trichotomies as "galant-learned," "elevated-plain," "high-middle-low," or "church-theater-chamber" styles attests to the legacy of rhetoric and its applicability to music of this period. Connecting learned style with rhetoric are several separate but related complexes of ideas: the idea of an older, antiquated style dependent upon strict rules; the idea of a musical *topos* or topic, already explored in Chapter 5; the idea of elevated style, as outlined in Chapter 2; and the idea of difficulty inherent in learnedness, and thus the propriety of taxing the understanding of the audience. Ultimately, the rhetoric of the learned style will invoke the sublime, to elucidate what I believe to be the real significance of this movement.

Analogies between rhetorical elements and matters of style and taste were pervasive in the eighteenth century. An important class of these analogies concerned the level of learning of the performer and audience and the extent to which rhetorical effects are "natural." For example, Leopold Mozart's violin treatise echoed Quintilian on the naturalness of rhetorical figures and their use even by the uneducated: noting that appoggiaturas are "demanded by Nature herself" to beautify a melody, Leopold continued, "in the same way the simplest peasant often uses figures of speech and metaphors without knowing it."[2] The related point that both educated and uneducated people ought to be able to understand one's speech or artwork is also rhetorically based: thus, Wolfgang Mozart's often-quoted remark in a letter of 28 December 1782 – that his subscription piano concertos "strike a mean between too difficult and too easy – here and there connoisseurs alone can derive satisfaction; the non-connoisseurs cannot fail to be pleased, though without knowing why" – appears to elaborate on Quintilian's more laconic sentence, "Thus our language will be approved by the learned and clear to the uneducated," as well as Aristotle's "The mean is most suitable."[3] Similarly, the famed contrapuntist Albrechtsberger wrote of the usefulness of double counterpoint that "the uninitiated are often delighted, without being able to comprehend the real source of that which affects them."[4]

Learned style as topic

The question of what can be comprehended by what kind of listener raises a more specific correlation between rhetoric and music, and brings us back to the idea of topics. Because the strict or learned style may be considered a topic, that is, a type of musical style intelligible to the late-eighteenth-century audience, this relationship is of particular interest. But what aspect of rhetoric subsumes topics? Is a topic, or *topos*, part of rhetorical invention (*inventio*), which seeks commonplaces (*loci topici*) as subject matter, or part of arrangement (*dispositio*), which orders the arguments into a coherent whole? Or is it part of style (*elocutio*), which chooses appropriate figurative language to clothe the subject, or part of performance or delivery (*pronuntiatio*), in which gesture and tone convey meaning and carry persuasive power? In fact, the array of topics of the later eighteenth century participates in all of these areas.

Yet the term "learned style" has been used rather loosely in published analyses, and requires clarification as a topic. It would be going too far to refer virtually to any kind of imitative texture, and especially motivic imitation, as learned style; Ratner defined learned style as "imitation, fugal or canonic, and contrapuntal composition, generally."[5] Giorgio Pestelli, in setting out the kinds of styles available to Mozart, distinguished between strict church-related counterpoint, or *stile osservato*, and "secular" counterpoint, an "imitative style within a regime of free conversation,"[6] a dichotomy similar to seventeenth-century formulations. Where do fugue and fugato fit into this bifurcated model? Those eighteenth-century writers who differentiated between galant and strict or learned style generally meant less, or more, rule-bound, respectively, especially in dissonance treatment.[7] To Albrechtsberger even a fugue itself can be galant (his "galantry fugue") if the episodes do not rework the subjects contrapuntally but present "tender and blandishing ideas . . . with runs and triplets, or with ideas from the theater and chamber style."[8] Within the realm of the "secular counterpoint" of late-eighteenth-century instrumental music, there are actually at least two broad categories of imitative texture: first, fugue, fugato, and related *stile legato* or *alla breve* textures; and second, imitation of motives of the kind that permeates, say, the first movement of Mozart's "Prague" Symphony.[9] Fugue may be further sub-categorized according to the rhythm and style of the subject: one may speak perhaps of *stile antico* and *stile moderno* fugues and fugatos.

Are all of these types of counterpoint "learned style?" Only the first category just mentioned – fugal imitation, *stile legato*, *alla breve* – maintains the sense of quotation or importation, whether of something consciously archaic or learned or "elevated." During the Austrian educational reforms of the 1770s and 1780s, a course of study in the practical as well as the rhetorical elements of Latin was advocated because, as Gratian Marx wrote in 1775, "Latin . . . is neither a dead language, nor a learned language, but the actual language of all religious and much state and even some civic business."[10] Precisely the same formula might apply to contemporaneous instruction in fugue. By the late eighteenth century, Latin, rhetoric, and fugue were all learned languages. Indeed, the teaching of rhetoric and the teaching of fugue or learned style present the same metaphoric relationship to their respective arts: a venerable, older practice to which lip service is paid and which dominates the educational system, but whose actual applications are increasingly narrow.

Motivic imitation, together with other thematic and motivic combinations, countermelodies, and development, is a broad category of "Classical counter-point," and is not necessarily a stylistic signifier on the same level as fugato, which is truly in the learned-style category. Such a specific topical identification further clarifies the status of fugue in rhetorical terms: it is part of *elocutio*, style, because it is a consciously artificial mode of display, an ornament – indeed, Albrechtsberger's counterpoint treatise of 1790 speaks of it in these terms.[11] And as an ornament of style – a figure – its primary purpose is to produce an effect on the listener. Forkel, in the wide-ranging introduction to his history of music, went so far as to claim that fugues are powerful because they can represent (and thus move) the emotions of many people at once, adding voices one by one just as in Nature, as opposed to puny arias with their single melodic line.[12] He thus used against Rousseau his very argument that fugues are unintelligible because several voices speaking at once are unintelligible; a fugue, Forkel countered, is not "the fruit of mere artist's pedantry, it is the fruit of Nature."[13]

70

Moreover, the two types of counterpoint described here as "learned" and "Classical" may be correlated with the two senses of "figure" set out in classical rhetoric. Quintilian, for example, stated that "In the first [sense] it is applied to any form in which thought is expressed, just as it is to bodies which, whatever their composition, must have some shape. In the second and special sense, in which it is called a *schema*, it means a rational change in meaning or language from the ordinary and simple form, . . . that which is poetically or rhetorically altered from the simple and obvious method of expression."[14] "Classical counterpoint" was an ordinary resource of style – a figure in the first sense – to Haydn and Mozart. Fugato passages, however, in their conscious allusions to an elevated and older practice, are the second kind, special rhetorically altered figures that enable the intellect to interact with the imaginative painting of inner feelings.[15] Appealing as it does to both intellect and imagination, learned style thus works particularly well in the peroration, the final part of the oration or piece in which arguments are summed up in a last attempt to secure the emotions of the audience. It is no accident that full-movement fugues appear most often as the second of a pair of movements and in finales.

Learned and galant

If fugue is emblematic of the learned style, both are emblematic of the elevated style, which in its turn may include the aesthetic category of "sublime." Writers on music often made opposites of learned and galant style, but the latter term was in wide use for so long and came to have such different implications, that it has become excessively problematized in recent scholarship.[16] To some modern writers, "galant" seems to be the same as "Classical" – the basically accessible musical style of the late eighteenth century. Certainly Einstein meant it this way in describing the "Jupiter" as a synthesis of learned and galant. To others, galant is virtually synonymous with "Pre-Classic" or simple and trivial. I would argue that "galant," which came to mean essentially the same as "free composition" and could include music on all stylistic levels, ought to lose its stigma. It is useful to us as part of the distinction made by Marpurg (galant-learned) which is not only worth making but also captures an essential feature of Mozart's style, especially, as we shall see, in his concern to attract different kinds of listeners. At the risk of oversimplifying, then, I suggest that everything that is not learned, in this period, is "galant," including "Classical" (or "galant") counterpoint.

This point becomes clearer when we examine pieces in which both styles are combined. Just as the elevated style is not always sublime, the learned style does not always appear in pieces of uniformly elevated tone. One of Mozart's most striking admixtures of styles, the finale of the G-major String Quartet dedicated to Haydn, K. 387 (1782), embodies two finales in one, a fugal finale and a racy, comic/galant, aggressively homophonic sonata finale. This movement seems almost the paradigm case of the mixing of comic and serious styles in Viennese music that so offended the Berlin critics from the 1760s on, and that was considered unacceptable by rhetoricians as well: a particularly clear example of this can be found in John of Garland's early thirteenth-century treatise, *De arte prosayca, metrica, et rithmica*: "There are six vices of composition . . . the mixing of comedy and tragedy in the same part of the work; unsuitable digressions; obscure brevity; unsuitable mixing of styles; improper mixing of subjects; and the use of endings not suitable to the type of writing."[17] Mozart's quartet finale scores a direct hit on virtually every one of these.

Mozart might have been working on this quartet when he wrote the letter to his father (already cited) of 28 December 1782; the quartet autograph is dated 31 December. In praising his concertos for appealing to the learned and less-learned in an audience, he spoke of their appropriate mean (*Mittelding*) between too difficult and too easy; he went on to deplore the overblown Denis text on Gibraltar, adding "The mean, [or middle ground], truth in all things, is known and valued no longer; to receive approval one has to write something so easy to understand that a coachman can sing it right off, or so incomprehensible that it pleases precisely because no rational person can understand it."[18] In the string quartet finale, Mozart juxtaposes the difficult learned style with the approachable galant. As Table 8.1 shows, every functional area in the sonata-form exposition is bifurcated, the first theme and bridge passage each into learned-galant, the second theme into fugue-double fugue, and the closing section into a chirpy, repetitive theme and cadence passage. Changes in tone occur with the suddenness of flicking a switch. Not until the development do the styles meet – the first fugue subject harmonized by the repeated notes of the closing theme as countersubject – and not until the coda do they resolve: the whole-note subject is given a galant final cadence. The styles otherwise remain discrete, each part of a rhetorical *antithesis* (Example 8.1 shows the double fugue 2b and closing Cl.a).

Or do the styles remain discrete? There are points of common ground between the antitheses: the learned bridge retains the eighth-note pattern of the galant 1b as a bass sequence; the double fugue 2b yields to a decorous trill cadence before the light-hearted closing. But only in the shortened recapitu-

Table 8.1. *String Quartet in G Major, K. 387/IV. Molto allegro*

EXPOSITION

First group (tonic)
1a   1   Learned style: fugal exposition, whole-note subject, syncopated
               countersubject
1b   17   Galant style: cadential passage, accompanied treble figuration

Bridge
Br.a   31   Learned style: syncopated seq. with susps.
Br.b   39   Galant style: chrom. cadence passage, repeated-note accompaniment

Second group (dominant)
2a   51   Learned style: fugal exposition, syncopated subject
2b   69   Learned style: double fugue on 1a and 2a

Closing (dominant)
Cl.a   91   Galant style: comic alternations of I and V, 4 + 4 repeated with
               varied rhythm
Cl.b 107   Galant style: chordal cadence passage

DEVELOPMENT
         124   imit. on asc. chrom. line
         143   1a theme, repeated-note accompaniment
         159   imit. of repeated notes
         171   retrans.

RECAPITULATION

First group (subdominant)
1b   175
Br.a 189
Br.b 198

Second group (tonic)
2b   209   ends with ♭VI accompanied subject and dance-like trans. ***

Closing (tonic)
Cl.a 235
Cl.b 251

CODA
         267   cf. development: imit. on asc. chrom. line
         282   subject harmonized (whole-note stretto)
         292   galant cadence

Example 8.1.   Mozart, String Quartet in G major, K. 387/IV,
double fugue on **1a** and **2a**; closing theme (**Cl.a**)

lation does Mozart actually reveal that the mean is not an appropriation of one style by the other but a process linking them.[19] The last statement in the double fugue is recast as a climactic treble subject in E♭ (♭VI) accompanied by a lively new rhythm which slowly wends its way across the dance floor to a cadence and the closing theme (Example 8.2). Thus, Mozart shows us the two extremes before revealing the middle ground; accommodation is possible through dance, the universal solvent. Never again, however, did he return to this rather uneasy accommodation between styles. When he next used a fugue as first theme, in the overture to *Die Zauberflöte*, its character was transformed by the comic, *stile moderno* qualities of a subject in quick repeated notes.

The oration as peroration: learned, galant, and sublime

The rhetorical status of the learned style in the "Jupiter" finale is entirely different from that of K. 387. First, unlike the vast majority of fugal finales in this period, it does not actually begin with the fugue.[20] Second, the whole-note theme, the main theme of the movement, is presented in both galant and learned guises, in the sections labelled 1A and 1B on Table 4.4 (p. 44), and as a homophonic theme it has an important sequel (x and x', the phrase beginning with repeated notes). Third, the galant style is not as unclouded

Example 8.2. Mozart, K. 387/IV, recapitulation:
end of **2b** and transition to **C1**.

here as in the quartet, because every theme and motive is treated contrapuntally (that is, with "Classical counterpoint") in the manner of the "Prague"
Symphony. Moreover, the ubiquitous motive **b**, with its fanfare dotted
rhythm and descending scale that concludes virtually every functional
segment of the piece (**1A, Br., C1.**, not to mention the development), is, after
its first appearance, always treated in stretto, creating a significant amount of
rhythmic disorder. Indeed, the resemblance between this motive and the
second theme (**d**, three half-notes and a descending scale pattern) is increased
at the stretto of the second theme that concludes the second group.[21] Exciting
performances of this movement exploit its stretto-induced confusion.

But the most significant rhetorical feature of the opening of the "Jupiter"
finale is that of its double beginning: the movement literally begins twice and,
given the tradition of fugal finales, in the "wrong" order. Mozart's method
of finding the mean yet again between accessibility and difficulty here requires
nothing less than the Ciceronian dual exordium, which is divided into the
introduction (*principium*) and the insinuation (*insinuatio*): "An introduction is
an address which directly and in plain language makes the auditor well-
disposed, receptive, and attentive. The insinuation is a speech which by
dissimulation and indirection unobtrusively steals into the mind of the
auditor."[22] Warren Kirkendale has suggested that preludes in chordal style

correspond to the first and imitative ricercars to the second type of opening; in the latter, the "voices creep in quietly one by one."[23] By cutting off the last bar of the square four-note subject (as at bar 39) Mozart also creates a subtle asymmetry to enhance this effect.

Why would Mozart need two exordia in this finale? The simple answer is: to prepare the listener for the dual stance of the movement vis-à-vis the textural norms of the day: the first section, with its thematic contrast (a–x, a–x', b), flourishes, and syncopated suspensions, anticipates a contrapuntally enriched sonata design, while the fugue (bar 36) looks forward to the fugal coda. But, because the two exordia treat the same theme, a middle ground cannot be found – the futile alternations of the development attest to this. In the recapitulation and coda Mozart must transcend both. The learned style here, in appearing to negate the opening – to create a fundamental conflict – functions as a signifier of the sublime, in particular the Kantian mathematical sublime described in Chapter 2.

Writers after Kant adapted his ideas on the sublime to music, and tried to come up with musical equivalents for overwhelming grandeur and enormous complexity. One of the best of these was Michaelis, who applied Kant's aesthetic theories to music generally. In a comment representative of late-eighteenth- and early-nineteenth-century thinking, he identified the sublime in music as arising either "by uniformity so great that it almost excludes variety" or "by too much diversity . . . (as in many polyphonic compositions . . .) [so that] the imagination cannot easily and calmly integrate the diverse ideas into a coherent whole without strain."[24] But the sublime in Mozart's music cannot be so easily pigeonholed.

Mozart was fully aware that people found his music difficult; in the "Jupiter" he seemed to magnify the difficulty to specific rhetorical ends, the full union of figures for intellect and imagination. In so doing, he captured the essence of the mathematical sublime. The three short segments in which this happens – the sublime must always be brief – are in the recapitulation and coda, and were all prepared by the dual exordium: the fate of the first theme; the closing theme based on the first theme's sequel (x); and the coda itself (marked with asterisks in Table 4.4). When, just after the beginning of the recapitulation, the tutti affirmation of the theme is called for, Mozart replaces it with a bizarrely dissonant series of restatements of the four notes, first ascending and then descending the scale, together with a learned-style countermelody (Example 8.3).

Why is this mathematical? Because the dissonances seem to increase exponentially to the point of not being aurally comprehensible, and because

Example 8.3.   Mozart, K. 551/IV, recapitulation:
dissonant passage (**1B**)

they keep increasing as the theme goes up and down in an unmotivated
sequence which calls into question every possible meaning that the theme has
previously suggested, especially in its parody of strict-style dissonance
treatment. The passage is disordered and obscure, massive and repetitious (all
terms that appear in discussions of the sublime). It is also fleeting: Mozart
magnifies the drama of magnitude by denying us the leisure to contemplate
it. Nothing better illustrates Mozart's rhetorical conception of form than his
recognition that the original fugue – his *insinuatio* – could not return here; it
had already played its rhetorical part.

   The second passage arises during the closing theme, and, because it is related
to the C-minor passage and F-minor/D♭-major passages in the first movement

Example 8.4. Mozart, K. 551/IV

a) exposition, closing theme (**Cl.A**)

b) "Mannheim cadence" (**Cl.B**)

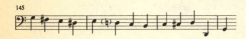

c) recapitulation, closing theme (**Cl.A**)

(at bars 81 and 269), provides a superb confirmation of the rhetorical effect of derivation identified as "epiphany" by Edward Cone.[25] In the exposition of the Finale, during the sudden turn to a C-minor chord in the closing section (bar 128, Example 8.4a), the pitch C is on top during the C-minor and subsequent C-major chords, and then moves into a quasi-cliché, a nod to what I call the "Mannheim cadence" (in brief at bars 133–5, more extended in bars 145–51, Example 8.4b). In the recapitulation, the comparable F-minor chord also has the pitch C on top, but this suddenly ascends to D♭ major in an ecstatic trajectory, identifying a sublime turn, creating bafflement and blockage, and finally exultation: a further ascent is needed before resolution (Example 8.4c). It should be noted that this theme is not in learned style, but that as part of the first theme in the exposition (**x**) it functioned always in opposition to the learned style. Lacking in the recapitulation of the first theme, then, this galant theme requires its own sublime turn.

Finally, the coda of the "Jupiter" finale – the most celebrated part of the entire symphony – is a peroration encapsulating and reversing the dual exordium, moving from contrapuntal chaos to the confident closure of the galant. For a frustratingly brief span, it is a simultaneous presentation of nearly every one of the many themes and motives of the movement (see Example 4.5): a double fugue on the first and second theme, a canon on every one of the important motives, a triumphant reassertion of the four-note theme, its measured tread present in every bar.[26] But the mass of simultaneously writhing fragments, at all rhythmic levels and in all instruments, with the relentless background of the four whole-notes, cannot be taken in. It reveals vistas of contrapuntal infinity. The coda thus creates a cognitive exhaustion born of sheer magnitude. It makes vivid the mathematical sublime.

In the principal recurring image for the sublime between the late seventeenth and the late eighteenth centuries, we may find an appropriate metaphor for the experience of this symphony.[27] As we have seen, the astonishing force of the sublime was likened to a thunderbolt, an image of nature, but it was also often personified: the orator and the artist were able to awe their audience just as did the great hurler of thunderbolts from Olympus – Jupiter himself.

Appendix

A. Oulibicheff (Ulïbïchev), "The 'Jupiter' Symphony of Mozart," *Dwight's Journal of Music* (Boston), vol. 27, no. 16 (26 October 1867), pp. 121–2. ("Translated from the German for this Journal.") Source: Oulibicheff, *Nouvelle Biographie de Mozart* (Moscow, 1843), vols. II and III.

We come now to Mozart's last and most perfect creations in the Symphony kind: the works in G minor and in C. They are almost twin sisters, for they were produced only a month apart. Although these sisters are incomparably beautiful, they differ none the less in features and in character. A dilettante of the eighteenth century would have compared the younger to Minerva, accompanied by Apollo and the Muses; and the older to Venus weeping over the death of Adonis; and he would have recognized in the one all the attributes of the heart, in the other all the gifts of the mind.

The man of all kinds, all expressions, all contrasts, has bequeathed to us a last work, in which instead of the elegiac mode (Symph. in G minor) with its most sorrowful outpourings, we find the Dithyramb raised to the highest pitch of splendor, of enthusiasm, of sublime Pindaric intoxication and bewilderment. The Symphony in C shows us what glorious inspirations lifted Mozart's soul from the things of to-day to a better morrow, in the midst of the sorrows which he has just related to us (in the G-minor), sorrows inseparable from a doomed and already wavering life, from which each of his masterworks took away with it a part, and of which already he began to feel the end so near.

One might believe that the Symphony in C had been designed to glorify some extraordinary event in the annals of the world, some exceedingly happy and ever to be remembered victory! The loud ringing pomp of the orchestra, which makes itself remarked from the ninth bar in all its might, decidedly denotes the joyfulness of victory as the ground character of the work; but the Theme, which precedes this outbreak of victorious joy, is double. It consists of a sort of proclamation or *fanfare*, upon which there follows a little questioning phrase in tied notes. That is the main thought, the fruitful theme, which by its developments impresses upon the great jubilation of the Allegro a quite peculiar stamp of spirituality and announces itself to the soul as a persistent striving after I know not what intellectual heights, which the poet burns to reach but which he only reaches toward the end of the Ode. There is nothing more majestic and more splendid than the expansions, transformations, and analyses of the two fragments of the theme. The one resounds like the cascade of a forest brook, which the echoes in multiplied tones repeat to the mountains; the other figure, ever pursuing, under different forms, the goal for which it strives, now dives under in the bass, now floats aloft upon the melody, and now, gathered up in a powerful *unisono*, it mounts and obstinately makes its way through the lists which are firmly held by the extreme voices of the orchestra and supported by the long-drawn tones of the trumpets. An inexpressible, sublime effect. The middle portion, one of the most beautiful examples of *worked* music, is for the greater part made out of an accessory thought. This is the precious, not to be forgotten song of the violins, with an accompaniment in *pizzicato*, which, first heard in the Dominant, now transposed into E-flat major and treated as a subject, here furnishes the contrapuntal matter. Toward the close, this song appears in the Tonic as melody with new charms.

Andante, F major, 3-4 time. Whether the slow *tempo* follows a piece of energetic or of sad expression, or comes in after the outburst of a jubilant enthusiasm, like the first Allegro of our Symphony, it always indicates that moment of repose, of rest, of enervation or of intermission, which succeeds a spell of strong emotional activity. Here the suspension of the Ode, the Andante, gives us the image of a tranquil blissfulness, the pure height of enchantment. The theme, full of the most ravishing expression, and as singable as a piece written for the voice, occupies less room than Mozart commonly allows to the initial thought, with its modulations, in the putting together of the piece; and this comes from the superabundance of accessory thoughts, the number and the peculiar euphony of the concurring motives. This multitude of fine melodic details, mingled with long passages of demisemiquavers and sextoles, these phrases self-multiplied in all their repetitions and imitations, spread over the piece a sort of twilight, while the ear loses itself with rapture, as the eye does in a thicket which the sunbeams penetrate perpendicularly, illuminating, enkindling and peopling it with a thousand fantastical forms. From time to time, though, some great opaque clouds obscure the blue of heaven. The soul feels the sting of a sudden pain, painful syncopations trouble the harmony, the Minor steps into the foreground and reigns through a succession of short-breathed and affrighted phrases; but these vapors without water, these unsubstantial shapes of terror, the humors of a moody wind, vanish as swiftly as they came. The sun prevails over all these impotent half-wills of the foul weather; his radiant face appears with the theme, and the heart soars anew amid the beams of unextinguishable bliss. Mozart must have been satisfied with his Andante; we too are satisfied, and very much so; though candidly we must confess that we prefer that in the G-minor Symphony.

After the composer has rested in this sentimental meditation, full of charm, his fiery lyrical spirit is enkindled anew and breaks forth with impetuous, lively humor in the *Minuet, Allegretto, 3-4*, which they commonly take *Allegro*. It is made after the technical pattern of the older one in G minor, apart from the difference of the ideas, which is very great. The same nimble, noisy motives fill the two parts of the piece; but in the first they are presented in a simple melody, and in the second, which is much longer and more interesting, the composer has submitted them to the difficult test of wonderful contrapuntal play, after which comes a *Coda* of the wind instruments, not less wonderful than that in the other Minuet. The Trio is a graceful prattle, cut short awhile by some energetic phrases in the Minor, in which the obstinate tone, the E, blown in the octave by the trumpets, produces the finest effect.

Who could count the abominations which the learned ones of that day might have found in the Finale to the Symphony in C? How the fearful fugue with four subjects must have heated their poor brains! This was neither BACH nor HANDEL, it was none of their acquaintance; it was MOZART. Where could they have found a measure for him, who had shattered their square and compass? Some of their criticisms have come down to us as monuments of their confusion; some fragments which we have cited elsewhere, will suffice to give an idea of the difference between the old fugue (strict and regular) and the free fugue of Mozart, which does not subject itself to the methodical periods of the class and admits mixture of style. When we spoke of unity with variety as essential conditions of the fugue, we recognized that variety involved two principles: canonical imitation and contrast of melodies. Bach had exhausted the first means; Mozart understood how to win an advantage from the second, which contributed more than all else to lend to music a new organization. Mozart, who was not a less sharp-sighted canonist than Bach, but who was far more inventive and incomparably bolder, wove into the contrapuntal web melodies so different from one another, that one hardly conceives it possible that they could legitimately stand side by side; and when the eye has finally convinced itself, one still asks whether it can satisfy the ear.

A pardonable doubt, which the exception soon turns to enthusiasm. This Finale consists of four themes, which surely do not look as if they were made to dwell together. Let the reader convince himself [example shows first four themes of Example 4.5, written consecutively]. At the end of the piece, the composer brings them all four forward, and the answer to no one of them is wanting. The union of imitation and contrast certainly could go no further.

With such modulation, full of boldness and of genius; with such freedom of style, such incredible power of combinations; with themes so opposite in character and outline; with an orchestral accompaniment, in fine, consisting of from fifteen to twenty voices and instrumented after Mozart's manner, the Fugue must naturally have expanded its effects and rendered itself applicable far beyond the utmost limits ever dreamed of by the contrapuntists old and new. The fugue is no longer the mere abstract expression of some sort of emotion; it can become picture, translate itself into action, paint a battle or anything that is positive, without any danger of falling into that kind of music which requires a programme.

To keep to our example, what then is the finale to the Symphony in C, which dazzles those who read and makes the hearer dizzy? It seems to me, that this *Allegro* is the sequel to the *Grave* (representing the emerging of Order out of Chaos) with which "The Creation" of HAYDN begins. Light has illumined the abyss; the laws of creation are in full force; suddenly the elements, indignant at the new yoke, attempt a revolution to win back the old anarchy. Fire, Air, Earth, and Water one by one desert their appointed places and commingle in the vortex, in which the germinating Order seems to sink forever; a sublime spectacle to contemplate, like every great rebellion of matter against mind, its ruler. But this propensity to relapse into chaos has been foreseen; it serves, like order itself, the final ends of the eternal wisdom. The elemental forces may melt in one inextricable mass (the fugued portions of the piece), but they hear a voice which calls to them: "Thus far and no farther," and in a moment all is disentangled, and the young universe comes forth victorious and beautiful from the midst of this frightful confusion (the portions composed in the melodic style upon the same motives).

Here we see the fugued style come out of the psychologically indefinite and abstract procession, within which it had so far confined itself, and by its union with the simple style, produce splendid analogies, to which neither the one nor the other could have attained singly. In this way Mozart seems to us the last word of the Flemish school, the primitive tendency of musical Art. Bach, who perfected the fugue, so far as it was possible within the strict limits and the partially conventional forms, which the contrapuntists of the seventeenth century had prescribed to him, lifted the style to a very lofty height of grandeur and of science. Our hero enhanced this grandeur and this science by the wonders of his orchestral accompaniment and by the expansion which he gave to the principles of contrast. He understood how to make the fugue in the highest degree melodious and expressive, while he made it free. The old scholastic mould broke in pieces in his hands, and out of its ruins sprang its last and richest treasure, the queen of fugues, the work of works, the overture to *Zauberflöte*.

We have recognized a material analogy, in this Finale, with the ways which Haydn has adopted in the Introduction to his *Creation*. But all musical resemblances of this sort necessarily have their roots in a psychological analogy, inasmuch as the phenomena of the soul always find their correspondences in the phenomena of the outward world; accordingly in this Finale we may find the triumph of Order in the final supremacy of a thought that wavers for a time amid the many and the formidable images besieging it at once. From lyrical enthusiasm the poet has passed into the state of ecstasy and clairvoyance; what he at first related, he now sees; his power of will, at first active and full of insight, becomes passive and mechanical; he seems to obey an influence from without, which subjugates, transports him, surrounds him with vast illusions and whispers to him words, of which he is the mere echo. The human event, which he has been glorifying, transforms itself into the *second sight* of the poet, with the whole series of causes that have induced it, with the whole chain of consequences that must spring out of it; the past, the present and the future appear to him united, yet clearly distinguishable, in this indivisible point in which they come in mutual contact, to reproduce each other and then die. The mind yields itself to contemplation of the divine origin and foreordination of events, of the motive springs and reactions, of forces and counter-forces, of the coöperation and the conflict of sympathetic and hostile influences, of the whole wonderful mechanism, in which at first it is aware of nothing but a vast, inexplicable confusion, resulting none the less, according to our first analogy, in moral order.

We see that nothing yields itself to interpretation more than the ideal meaning of pure music, and especially the meaning of a Fugue. Every one can explain it to himself in his own way, according to the idea or the image which the hearings may chance to awaken in him. But whatever interpretation one may give to the Finale of our Symphony, all will agree in one thing: that it will dazzle those who see it (in notes), and that it must make dizzy those who hear it; a dizziness of wonder and enthusiasm. One must needs hear this music to believe it possible; it seems not to be, if studied with the eyes.

An impartial but timid criticism might perhaps ask, whether Mozart has not misused his genius in this singular composition, in order, so to say, to be gigantic and sublime; whether we do not find in it an excess of boldness and transporting power, an excess of combinations and figures, of learned harmony and canon, a monstrous largeness in the laying out of the plan and details of the piece, a taxing of attention even to weariness, an overloading for the ear, and now and then an obvious and culpable contempt of the rules which still stand in force? The reader may be sure we would refuse, with the whole force of our conviction and our musical sympathies, to join in such a judgment. Does not this music give one all he can properly demand of it? Is it not in fact an exaltation of the tripod, which seems almost like delirium, denoting a degree of intellectual clairvoyance foreign to the normal state of man? Is it not that tremendous and eccentric power of thought, that shatters all known forms of speech, to recombine them in new words, new constructions, like the things themselves which the poet has to say to one? Is it not, in a word, the Dithyramb raised by music to its highest efficacy! In our view the Fugue in C is the masterwork of Mozart in the Symphonic kind and the highest expression of the kind itself, *the highest standpoint* [*der höchste Standpunkt*, given in German even in the original French edition]. It is also the last effort of our hero in this branch of Art. Since Mozart could no farther go, he composed no more Symphonies, and left to his followers the glory of lifting this kind even to the Drama, and of characterizing their productions by descriptive titles which the hearers never could have thought of.

Notes

Preface

1. *A Mozart Pilgrimage. Being the Travel Diaries of Vincent and Mary Novello in the Year 1829*, transcribed and compiled by Nerina Medici di Marignano, ed. Rosemary Hughes (London, 1955), p. 99. The earliest appearances of the name were first brought to light by A. Hyatt King in *Mozart in Retrospect: Studies in Criticism and Bibliography* (Oxford, 1955, 3rd rev. edn., 1970); he also uncovered the 1823 Clementi edition, given as the frontispiece to that book, the earliest known with the title "Jupiter."
2. Letter of 30 December 1780, trans. in Emily Anderson, *The Letters of Mozart and His Family*, 3rd edn. (New York, 1985), no. 383, p. 701. Leopold had twice urged his son to finish the third act, using the same Latin expression; cf. his letters of 18 December and 25 December 1780 (Anderson nos. 377a, p. 692 and 380, p. 696).
3. *Mozart-Jahrbuch 1975: Mozart-Bibliographie*, with periodic updates; Neal Zaslaw, *Mozart's Symphonies: Context, Performance Practice, Reception* (Oxford, 1989), p. 442 n. 175. The only monographs devoted solely to Symphony No. 41 are Johann Nepomuk David, *Die Jupiter-Symphonie: Eine Studie über die thematisch-melodischen Zusammenhänge* (Göttingen, 1953), and Stefan Kunze, *Wolfgang Amadeus Mozart: Sinfonie in C-dur KV 551, Jupiter-Sinfonie*, Meisterwerke der Musik, L (Munich, 1988).
4. Some scholars would argue for the inclusion of symphonies going back to the C-major No. 34, K. 338, as does Felix Salzer, who stated "the still habitual designation of only Mozart's last three symphonies as outstanding works reflects a serious misjudgment" ("The Variation Movement of Mozart's Divertimento K. 563," *Music Forum* 5 [1980], 314n).

1 The symphony in Mozart's Vienna

1. See Mary Sue Morrow, *Concert Life in Haydn's Vienna: Aspects of a Developing Musical and Social Institution* (New York, 1989); Elaine R. Sisman, "Haydn's Theater Symphonies," *Journal of the American Musicological Society* 43 (1990), 292–352; Neal Zaslaw, "Mozart, Haydn, and the *Sinfonia da chiesa*," *Journal of Musicology* 1 (1982), 95–124.
2. Cited in Neal Zaslaw, "Toward the Revival of the Classical Orchestra," *Proceedings of the Royal Musical Association* 103 (1976–7), 169. Mozart's own account, given in a letter to his father of 29 March 1783 (Anderson no. 484, p. 843), is chattier, identifying performers and titles.
3. Mozart does not specify which movements were performed at the beginning of the concert, only the finale at the end. Zaslaw, "Revival," suggests that only the first three movements were performed.
4. See László Somfai, "The London Revision of Haydn's Instrumental Style," *Proceedings of the Royal Musical Association* 100 (1973–4), 166.
5. Zaslaw, *Mozart's Symphonies*, p. viii. He points out that "*Gebrauchsmusik*, when divorced from its original setting, loses some of its meaning."
6. Heinrich Christoph Koch, *Versuch einer Anleitung zur Composition*, 3 vols. (Rudolstadt and Leipzig, 1782–93; rpt. Hildesheim, 1969); trans. Nancy K. Baker, *Introductory Essay on*

Composition (New Haven and London, 1983). See also Baker, "Heinrich Koch's Description of the Symphony," *Studi musicali* 9 (1980), 303–16.

7. Michael Broyles, "The Two Instrumental Styles of Classicism," *Journal of the American Musicological Society* 36 (1983), 220. The aesthetic character of symphonies will be taken up in Chapter 2.

8. Heinrich Christoph Koch, *Musikalisches Lexikon* (Frankfurt, 1802; rpt. Hildesheim, 1964), s.v. "Variazionen, Variazioni." He did not describe the difference between pieces for such "private enjoyment" and works destined for the public.

9. Andrew Steptoe, *The Mozart-Da Ponte Operas: The Cultural and Musical Background to Le nozze di Figaro, Don Giovanni, and Così fan tutte* (Oxford, 1988), pp. 85–6.

10. Morrow, *Concert Life*, p. 93; Marcel Brion, *Daily Life in the Vienna of Mozart and Schubert*, trans. Jean Stewart (New York, 1962), p. 18.

11. Volkmar Braunbehrens, *Mozart in Vienna, 1781–1791*, trans. Timothy Bell (New York, 1989), p. 42.

12. Letter to his father of 3 March 1784; Anderson no. 505, pp. 869–70.

13. Letters of 4 and 22 January 1783, Anderson nos. 477 and 480, pp. 835 and 838.

14. Morrow, *Concert Life*, p. 15.

15. On the kinds of works and their scoring preferred by Mozart for different performing circumstances, see Linda Faye Ferguson, "*Col Basso* and *Generalbass* in Mozart's Keyboard Concertos: Notation, Performance Theory, and Practice" (Ph.D. diss., Princeton University, 1983), and Christoph Wolff, "Über kompositionsgeschichtlichen Ort und Aufführungspraxis der Klavierkonzerte Mozarts," *Mozart-Jahrbuch 1984/5*, 91–3.

16. See A. Peter Brown, "The Symphonies of Carlo d'Ordonez: a contribution to the history of Viennese instrumental music during the second half of the eighteenth century," *Haydn Yearbook* 12 (1981), 9 and Plate 3. The Society itself was founded in 1771.

17. Morrow, *Concert Life*, pp. 49–64. Dexter Edge, in a far-reaching critique of Morrow's book, suggests other kinds of public concerts, including outdoor serenades and concerts in churches: he also substantially enlarges her concert calendar, promising more detail in a future study. See his Review Article on her book in *Haydn Yearbook* 17 (1992), 108–66.

18. Karl Dittersdorf, *The Autobiography of Karl Dittersdorf, Dictated to His Son*, trans. A. D. Coleridge (London, 1896; rpt. New York, 1970), p. 256. An anecdote about the first performances led Dittersdorf to recount in detail a conversation with the Emperor in which he touched on the relative merits of Haydn and Mozart, one of the most celebrated items in the book. The second set of six Ovid symphonies is lost.

19. His famous letter to the monastery in Lower Austria for which he had written the cantata *Applausus* in 1768 shows him to have been both insecure and defensive about composing for unknown performers, listeners, and space: "Finally I ask everyone, and especially the musicians, for the sake of my reputation as well as their own, to be as diligent as possible: if I have perhaps not guessed the taste of these gentlemen, I am not to be blamed for it, for I know neither the persons nor the place, and that fact that they were concealed from me really made my work very difficult." See Haydn, *Collected Correspondence and London Notebooks*, trans. and ed. H. C. Robbins Landon (London, 1959), p. 11, quoted in Landon, *Haydn: Chronicle and Works* (London and Bloomington, 1978), II, p. 148.

20. According to Paul Nettl, the concerts were open only to Masons and were held in the context of Masonic ritual: "The members of the orchestra appeared in embroidered suits with lace cuffs and wore ceremonial swords and cocked hats." See Nettl, *Mozart and Masonry* (New York, 1957), p. 41.

21. For more on K. 477, see Philippe A. Autexier, "Wann wurde die Maurerische Trauermusik uraufgeführt?," *Mozart-Jahrbuch 1984/5*, 6–8; he claims that the original version (which he calls the *Master Music*) had a chorus, whereas the funeral-music version omitted the chorus. See the section on Freemasonry written by Autexier in *The Mozart Compendium*, ed. H. C. Robbins Landon (New York, 1990), pp. 132–4.

22. All three listed in Autexier, "Freemasonry," in *Mozart Compendium*, ed. Landon, p. 133; the first two also in Otto Erich Deutsch, *Mozart: A Documentary Biography* (Stanford, 1965), pp. 254, 256–7. Deutsch does not mention the Archduke's marriage; that information appears in H. C. Robbins Landon, *Mozart: The Golden Years, 1781–1791* (New York, 1989), p. 191, which does not mention the concert. These concerts are not listed in the Private Concert Calendar (Appendix 2) of Morrow, *Concert Life*.
23. Deutsch, *Mozart*, p. 257. See also Philippe A. Autexier, "La Musique Maçonnique," *Dix-Huitième Siècle* 19 (1987), 97–104. Landon traces the genealogy of the Esterházys, showing Johann to be Johann Baptist, rather than Johann Nepomuk Esterházy, in *Mozart: The Golden Years*, pp. 114–19.
24. Charles Burney, *An Eighteenth-Century Musical Tour in Central Europe and the Netherlands. Dr. Burney's Musical Tours in Europe*, ed. Percy A. Scholes, II (London, 1959), pp. 75, 77–8, 111, and *passim*; Nicolai and others are quoted by Morrow, *Concert Life*, pp. 143–4.
25. Albert Christoph Dies, *Biographische Nachrichten von Joseph Haydn* (Vienna, 1810), trans. Vernon Gotwals in *"Haydn: Two Contemporary Portraits"* (Madison, 1968), pp. 129–30.
26. The programs are given in Landon, *Haydn Chronicle*, III, *passim*.
27. Morrow, *Concert Life*, p. 142.
28. See Sisman, "Haydn's Theater Symphonies," pp. 303–5.
29. Georg Joseph Vogler, *Betrachtungen der Mannheimer Tonschule* (Mannheim, 1778–81), I, p. 52, paraphrased by Floyd Grave in *In Praise of Harmony: The Teachings of Abbé Georg Joseph Vogler* (Lincoln, Neb., 1987), pp. 98–9.
30. Zaslaw discusses the "frame," briefly, in *Mozart's Symphonies*, p. 525; in stating that nothing has been written on frames in music, he has apparently overlooked the first chapter of Edward T. Cone, *Musical Form and Musical Performance* (New York, 1968): "The Picture and the Frame: The Nature of Musical Form."
31. Contemporary descriptions often focused on the quality of the wind players, and some orchestras made do with "dilettante" musicians for the most part but required professionals for the winds; a notice to this effect from 1803 is quoted in Morrow, *Concert Life*, p. 15.
32. Morrow, *Concert Life*, pp. 154–5; the statistic comes from the seventy concerts for which full information survives. She notes that Mozart was second in frequency to Haydn, and that after 1800, Cherubini and Beethoven dominated: "no other composer ever approached any of these four in terms of frequency of performance" (p. 156).
33. List compiled from the concert calendars in Morrow, *Concert Life*, Appendices 1 and 2.
34. The minuet of the C-major Symphony, No. 34, K. 338, was torn from the autograph, leaving only a fragment; see Zaslaw, *Mozart's Symphonies*, p. 361.
35. David P. Schroeder, *Haydn and the Enlightenment* (Oxford, 1990); Mark Evan Bonds, "Haydn's False Recapitulations and the Perception of Sonata Form in the Eighteenth Century" (Ph.D. diss., Harvard University, 1988).
36. This point is discussed in Chapter 4.
37. Mozart taught minuet-composition to Thomas Attwood, as well as to his other pupils like Barbara Ployer; treatises of the period like those by Riepel and Koch all began their instruction with the minuet. See Daniel Heartz, "Thomas Attwood's Lessons in Composition with Mozart," *Proceedings of the Royal Musical Association* 100 (1973–4), 175–83; Elaine R. Sisman, "Small and Expanded Forms: Koch's Model and Haydn's Music," *Musical Quarterly* 62 (1982), 444–78.
38. See Malcolm S. Cole, "The Rondo Finale: Evidence for the Mozart–Haydn Exchange?," *Mozart-Jahrbuch 1968–70*, 242–56; Stephen Fisher, "Sonata Procedures in Haydn's Symphonic Rondo Finales of the 1770s," in *Haydn Studies*, ed. Jens Peter Larsen, Howard Serwer, and James Webster (New York, 1981), pp. 481–7.
39. See n. 7.

2 Grand style and sublime in eighteenth-century aesthetics

1. See Erich Reimer, "Die Polemik gegen das Virtuosenkonzert im 18. Jahrhundert," *Archiv für Musikwissenschaft* 30 (1973), 235–44.
2. Johann Abraham Peter Schulz, "Symphonie," in Johann Georg Sulzer, *Allgemeine Theorie der schönen Künste*, 4 vols. in 2 (Leipzig, 1771–4), trans. slightly modified from the one given by Bathia Churgin in "The Symphony as Described by J. A. P. Schulz: A Commentary and Translation," *Current Musicology* 29 (1980), 7–16.
3. Koch, *Versuch* and *Musikalisches Lexikon*; Jean-Jacques Rousseau, *Dictionnaire de musique* (Paris, 1768; rpt. Hildesheim, 1968); trans. William Waring as *A Complete Dictionary of Music* (2nd edn., London, 1779; rpt. New York, 1975); Nicholas Framery, Pierre Ginguené, and Jérôme-Joseph de Momigny, *Encyclopédie méthodique: Musique*, 2 vols. (Paris, 1792–1818; rpt. New York, 1971).
4. Franz Xaver Niemetschek, *Leben des K. K. Kapellmeisters Wolfgang Gottlieb Mozart* (Prague, 1798), ed. Jost Perfahl as *Ich kannte Mozart* (Munich, 1984), p. 27; my translation.
5. For sources, see Brian Vickers, *In Defence of Rhetoric* (Oxford, 1988), pp. 80–2.
6. Interestingly, the treatise by Demetrius, *On Style*, finds four styles, differently divided: the "plain," the "elevated," the "elegant," and the "forcible." But for the two "opposites" – plain and elevated are on different levels – any may be combined with any other. See Demetrius, *On Style*, trans. W. Rhys Roberts, rev. edn., Loeb Classical Library (Cambridge, Mass., 1932), II.36, p. 323.
7. Forkel, *Allgemeine Geschichte der Musik* (Leipzig, 1788–1801), I, p. 44.
8. Fugue and learned style will be taken up in Chapter 8. On the meters and dance-types that form a spectrum from "ecclesiastical" to "terrestrial," see Wye J. Allanbrook, *Rhythmic Gesture in Mozart: Le Nozze di Figaro and Don Giovanni* (Chicago, 1983), p. 22. The term "sublime" was also used to describe sacred choral music and fugue.
9. This discussion of rhetoric is based on my book *Haydn and the Classical Variation* (Cambridge, Mass., 1993), ch. 2, "The Rhetoric of Variation."
10. See Hermann Meyer, "Schillers philosophische Rhetorik," in *Zart Empirie* (Stuttgart, 1963); John H. Smith, *The Spirit and Its Letter: Traces of Rhetoric in Hegel's Philosophy of Bildung* (Ithaca and London, 1988). On Leopold Mozart's education, see Adolf Layer, *Eine Jugend in Augsburg – Leopold Mozart 1719–1737* (Augsburg, c. 1974). And C. F. D. Schubart read Quintilian, as reported in *Schubart's Leben und Gesinnungen von ihm selbst, im Kerker aufgesetzt* (Stuttgart, 1791–3; rpt. Leipzig, 1980), I, p. 92. Important recent histories of rhetoric include George A. Kennedy, *Classical Rhetoric and Its Christian and Secular Tradition from Ancient to Modern Times* (Chapel Hill, 1980) and Brian Vickers, *In Defence of Rhetoric*. See also Ursula Stötzer, *Deutsche Redekunst im 17. und 18. Jahrhundert* (Halle, 1962). Though the course of study called "rhetoric" did not appear in the curriculum until the sixth year, rhetorical concepts were included in studies of grammar and literature undertaken in preceding years. See Fritz Keller, "Rhetorik in der Ordenschule," in *Die österreichische Literatur: ihr Profil an der Wende vom 18. zum 19. Jahrhundert (1750–1830)*, ed. Herbert Zeman (*Jahrbuch für österreichische Kulturgeschichte* 7–9 [1977–9]), p. 57.
11. As George J. Buelow put it, "The humanistic basis of education aspiring to teach every student the art of rhetorical eloquence permeated musical thought for centuries"; see "The *Loci Topici* and Affect in Late Baroque Music: Heinichen's Practical Demonstration," *Music Review* 27 (1966), 161–76, at 161. Among the principal modern surveys on rhetoric and music are Hans-Heinrich Unger, *Die Beziehungen zwischen Musik und Rhetorik im 16.–18. Jahrhundert* (Würzburg, 1941); Willibald Gurlitt, "Musik und Rhetorik," *Helicon* 5 (1943), 67–86; Rolf Dammann, *Der Musikbegriff im deutschen Barock* (Cologne, 1967), pp. 93–180. The most valuable recent study is Mark Evan Bonds, *Wordless Rhetoric: Musical Form and the Metaphor of the Oration* (Cambridge, Mass., 1991). Buelow includes an extensive bibliography of more

specialized studies in "Rhetoric and Music," *The New Grove Dictionary of Music and Musicians*, ed. Stanley Sadie (London, 1980), XV, pp. 793–803.

12. Johann Mattheson, *Der vollkommene Capellmeister* (Hamburg, 1739; facs. Kassel, 1969), Part II, ch. 14, pars. 1–25; Johann Adolph Scheibe, *Compendium Musices Theoretico-practicum, das ist Kurzer Begriff derer nöthigsten Compositions-Regeln* (c. 1728), ed. Peter Benary as the appendix to *Die deutsche Kompositionslehre des 18. Jahrhundert* (Leipzig, 1960), p. 75; Friedrich Wilhelm Marpurg, in the introduction to his *Anfangsgründe der theoretischen Musik* (Leipzig, 1757; facs. New York, 1966); Johann Nikolaus Forkel, *Allgemeine Geschichte der Musik* (Leipzig, 1788–1801), I, p. 39. See also Leonard Ratner, *Classic Music: Expression, Form, and Style* (New York, 1980), pp. 31–206.

13. Seventeenth-century writers include Joachim Burmeister, *Musica poetica* (Rostock, 1606; facs. Kassel, 1955); Christoph Bernhard, *Tractatus compositionis augmentatus*, ed. in Joseph Müller-Blattau, *Die Kompositionslehre Heinrich Schützens in der Fassung seines Schülers Christoph Bernhard* (Kassel, 1926); trans. Walter Hilse, "The Treatises of Christoph Bernhard," *Music Forum* 3 (1973), 1–196; Andreas Herbst, *Musica poetica* (Nürnberg, 1643). Twentieth-century writers include Arnold Schering, "Die Lehre von der musikalischen Figuren," *Kirchen-Musikalisches Jahrbuch* 21 (1908), 106–14; Heinz Brandes, *Studien zur musikalischen Figurenlehre im 16. Jahrhundert* (Berlin, 1935); Gurlitt, "Music und Rhetorik"; Unger, *Beziehungen zwischen Musik und Rhetorik*; Manfred Bukofzer, "Allegory in Baroque Music," *Journal of the Warburg and Courtauld Institutes* 3 (1939–40), 1–21. See the bibliographies in Buelow, "Rhetoric and Music," and in his "Music, Rhetoric, and the Concept of the Affections: A Selective Bibliography," *Notes* 30 (1973–4), 250–9.

14. Peter Williams, "The Snares and Delusions of Musical Rhetoric: Some Examples from Recent Writings on J. S. Bach," in *Alte Musik: Praxis und Reflexion*, ed. Peter Reidemeister and Veronika Gutmann (Winterthur, 1983), pp. 230–40; Vickers, "Figures of Rhetoric/Figures of Music?," *Rhetorica* 2 (1984), 1–44. See also David Schulenberg, "Musical Expression and Musical Rhetoric in the Keyboard Works of J. S. Bach," paper delivered at the Annual Meeting of the American Musicological Society, Vancouver, 1985; Maria Rika Maniates, "Music and Rhetoric: Faces of Cultural History in the Renaissance and Baroque," *Israel Studies in Musicology* 3 (1983), 44–69.

15. In an interesting recent study, Daniel Harrison ("Rhetoric and Fugue: An Analytical Application," *Music Theory Spectrum* 12 [1990], 1–42) suggests a retrieval of primary (persuasive) rhetoric to musical analysis rather than the secondary (formal) rhetoric applied by such writers as Gregory Butler in "Fugue and Rhetoric," *Journal of Music Theory* 21 (1977), 49–110. See also the very detailed and historically persuasive applications by Ursula Kirkendale ("The Source for Bach's *Musical Offering*: The *Institutio oratoria* of Quintilian," *Journal of the American Musicological Society* 33 [1980], 88–141) and Alan Street ("The Rhetorico-Musical Structure of the 'Goldberg' Variations: Bach's *Clavier-Übung* IV and the *Institutio oratoria* of Quintilian," *Music Analysis* 6 [1987], 89–131).

16. Vickers, *In Defence of Rhetoric*, p. 105.

17. See Sisman, *Haydn and the Classical Variation*, ch. 2. The text of the letter is given in *Joseph Haydn. Gesammelte Briefe und Aufzeichnungen*, ed. Dénes Bartha (Kassel, 1965), pp. 76–8; trans. in Landon, *Haydn Chronicle*, II, pp. 397–9. On the *ars dictaminis*, see James J. Murphy, *Rhetoric in the Middle Ages* (Berkeley and Los Angeles, 1974), pp. 194–268. The autobiography of C. P. E. Bach also contains, toward the end, a discussion of the shortcomings of critics. See William S. Newman, "Emanuel Bach's Autobiography," *Musical Quarterly* 51 (1965), 363–72.

18. See especially the letters of "before 17 June 1788" (Anderson no. 554, pp. 915–16) and 12 July 1789 (Anderson no. 567, pp. 929–31). See also Wolfgang Hildesheimer, *Mozart*, trans. Marion Faber (New York, 1983), pp. 19–25.

19. The mix of social classes within the lodges may have made rhetoric a kind of rank-free neutralizing force. For the percentages of the different groups in the Viennese lodges of this period, see Eva Huber, "Zur Sozialstruktur der Wiener Logen im Josephinischen

Jahrzehnt," in *Aufklärung und Geheimgesellschaften: Zur politischen Function und Sozialstruktur der Freimaurerlogen im 18. Jahrhundert*, ed. Helmut Reinalter (Munich, 1989), pp. 173–87.

20. The oration at Haydn's initiation is translated in Joachim Hurwitz, "Joseph Haydn and the Freemasons," *Haydn Yearbook* 16 (1985), 93–5.

21. Quintilian, XII.x.65, cited in David B. Morris, *The Religious Sublime: Christian Poetry and Critical Tradition in 18th-Century England* (Lexington, Ky., 1972), p. 15.

22. The modern reception of sublime properly begins with the translation by Nicolas Boileau [-Despréaux] of 1674, *Traité du Sublime ou de Merveilleux dans le Discours Traduit du Grec de Longin*. See Samuel Monk, *The Sublime: A Study of Critical Theories in XVIII-Century England* (1935; Ann Arbor, 1960), ch. 2.

23. Longinus, *On the Sublime*, trans. and ed. T. S. Dorsch in *"Classical Literary Criticism: Aristotle, Horace, Longinus"* (Middlesex, 1965), ch. 9, p. 109.

24. Cited in Frances Ferguson, "The Sublime of Edmund Burke, or the Bathos of Experience," *Glyph* 8 (1981), 63. As the critic Neil Hertz recently put it: "what he is moved to produce is not merely an analysis illustrative of the sublime but further figures for it." (*The End of the Line: Essays on Psychoanalysis and the Sublime* [New York, 1985], p. 8.)

25. Longinus, *On the Sublime*, ch. 8, p. 108.

26. Kennedy, *Classical Rhetoric*, p. 113.

27. Ibid., p. 226.

28. Gilbert Highet, *The Classical Tradition: Greek and Roman Influences on Western Literature* (Oxford, 1949), pp. 221, 224. He points out that until the nineteenth century their stanzaic and metrical structure was not well understood (pp. 222–4). An excerpt from the ode by Horace that praises Pindar is quoted by Carl Dahlhaus, *Ludwig van Beethoven: Approaches to His Music*, trans. Mary Whittall (Oxford, 1991), p. 72.

29. Boileau, *L'Art poétique* (1674), quoted by Highet, *Classical Tradition*, p. 224.

30. See Gernot Gruber, "Johann August Apel und eine Diskussion um Ästhetik der Sinfonie im frühen 19. Jahrhundert," in *Studien zur Instrumentalmusik: Lothar Hoffmann-Erbrecht zum 60. Geburtstag*, ed. Anke Bingmann, Klaus Hortschansky, and Winfried Kirsch (Tutzing, 1988), pp. 261–83; Dittersdorf, *Autobiography*, p. 253.

31. Jackson, *Observations on the State of Music in London*, quoted in Zaslaw, *Mozart's Symphonies*, p. 354.

32. Dating in Walter John Hipple, Jr., *The Beautiful, The Sublime, and the Picturesque in Eighteenth-Century British Aesthetic Theory* (Carbondale, 1957), p. 122.

33. Hugh Blair, *Lectures on Rhetoric and Belles-Lettres* (Edinburgh, 1783), pp. 47–8. Blair goes on to discuss beauty, the "next highest pleasure of the imagination," which can be enjoyed for a much longer period of time than sublimity because of the "agreeable serenity" it produces, and can as well be applied to a greater variety of objects, from a tree to a mathematical theorem (pp. 49–50).

34. Anderson no. 476, p. 833. This letter is often quoted for its remarks on Mozart's subscription concertos, K. 414, 413, and 415; see Chapter 8.

35. Letter to his father of 19 October 1782, Anderson no. 471, p. 828. A facsimile of the sketch (K. 386d) appears in Otto Jahn, *Life of Mozart* (1865), trans. Pauline D. Townsend (London, 1891; rpt. New York, 1970), II.

36. Denis is identified as a member of the lodge "Zur wahren Eintracht," which was under the direction of Ignaz von Born, in Nettl, *Mozart and Masonry* , p. 13. He published "Die Lieder Sineds des Barden" (Vienna, 1772) in an attempt to bring "Ossians Geist" to present-day events and rulers, in such poems as "Theresia die Fürstinn," "Theresia die Gattin," "Theresia die Mutter," "Theresia die Kriegerinn," "Theresia die Fromme," "Theresia die Weise," "Theresia die Gütige," and so on. The standard biography remains Paul von Hofmann-Wellenhof, *Michael Denis: Ein Beitrag zur Deutsch-Oesterreichischen Literaturgeschichte des XVIII. Jahrhunderts* (Innsbruck, 1881). See also Keller, "Rhetorik in der Ordensschule" (see n. 10), and *Joseph Haydn und die Literatur seiner Zeit*, ed. Herbert Zeman (*Jahrbuch für*

Österreichische Kulturgeschichte, 6 [1976]), *passim*. Denis corresponded with such luminaries as Klopstock, Bodmer, Gleim, Ramler, Weisse, and Nicolai, and even received letters for Ignaz von Born, the Viennese Masonic leader, in 1774. See *Michael's [sic] Denis Literarischer Nachlass*, ed. Joseph Friedrich Freyherrn von Retzer (Vienna, 1801).

37. See Christoph Wolff, "Mozart's *Messiah*: The Spirit of Handel from van Swieten's Hands," in *Music and Civilization: Essays in Honor of Paul Henry Lang*, ed. Edmond Strainchamps and Maria Rika Maniates (New York, 1984), pp. 1–14.

38. Letter of 21 March 1789, quoted in Georg Nikolaus von Nissen, *Biographie W. A. Mozarts* (1828; rpt. Hildesheim, 1984), p. 540. The authenticity of this letter is in doubt. Niemetschek's 1798 biography had referred to the "erhabenen Händel," and had cited the same; see *Leben des k. k. Kapellmeister Mozart*, pp. 30–1.

39. See Ludwig Finscher, "Bach in the Eighteenth Century," in *Bach Studies*, ed. Don O. Franklin (Cambridge, 1990), p. 295; Charles Burney, *A General History of Music from the Earliest Ages to the Present Period*, ed. Frank Mercer (New York, 1957), II, p. 98, cited in William Weber, "The Intellectual Bases of the Handelian Tradition, 1759–1800," *Proceedings of the Royal Musical Association* 108 (1981/82), 108.

40. Mainwaring, *Memoirs of the Life of the Late George Frederick Handel* (1760), p. 168, cited in Weber, "Handelian Tradition," p. 111.

41. Friedrich Rochlitz, "Anecdoten aus Mozarts Leben," *Allgemeine musikalische Zeitung* 1 (1799), col. 115. Mozart ostensibly made this remark after he had arranged Handel's *Acis and Galatea* and *Messiah*. Rochlitz's remark found its way into the biography by Edward Holmes, *The Life of Mozart including his Correspondence* (London, 1845; rpt. with a new introduction by Percy M. Young, New York, 1979, rpt. with a new introduction by Christopher Hogwood, London, 1991), and Jahn's *Life of Mozart*, II, p. 416. I am indebted to David Wright for turning my attention to the Jahn citation.

42. Van Swieten's instructions to Haydn are translated in Landon, *Haydn Chronicle*, IV, p. 351. An important study by Hans-Jürgen Horn connects this advice with the sublime ("FIAT LUX: Zum kunsttheoretischen Hintergrund der 'Erschaffung' des Lichtes in Haydns Schöpfung," *Haydn-Studien* 3 [1974], 65–84). James Webster kindly shared with me a paper he presented on "Haydn's *Creation* and the Musical Sublime" at a symposium on *The Creation* at the University of North Carolina at Chapel Hill, November, 1991.

43. Edmund Burke, *A Philosophical Enquiry into the Origin of Our Ideas of the Sublime and Beautiful*, 2nd edn. (1759), ed. James T. Boulton (Notre Dame, Ind. and London, 1968; first published 1958).

44. Ibid., pp. 57–9.

45. Ibid., pp. 113–17; p. 124 has a direct comparison of beauty and sublimity.

46. Letter of 29 November 1780; Anderson no. 365, p. 674.

47. Anderson, no. 382, 29 December 1780, p. 700.

48. On the various versions of *Idomeneo*, see the foreword by Daniel Heartz to his edition in the *Neue Mozart Ausgabe*, II/5/11. Ironically, the shortest version of the oracle is the only one not given in John Eliot Gardiner's CD recording on Archiv because he believes it is "too short" to make an appropriate effect.

49. Deutsch, *Mozart*, p. 341, from the *Dramaturgische Blätter*, Frankfurt, 1789.

50. Jean-François Lyotard, "The Sublime and the Avant-Garde," in *The Lyotard Reader*, ed. Andrew Benjamin (Oxford and Cambridge, Mass., 1989), pp. 198–9.

51. Ronald Paulson, *Representations of Revolution (1789–1820)* (New Haven, 1983), p. 7.

52. Zaslaw, *Mozart's Symphonies*, pp. 529–31.

53. Paul Guyer, *Kant and the Claims of Taste* (Cambridge, Mass., 1979), p. 500.

54. Immanuel Kant, *Critique of Judgment*, trans. J. H. Bernard (London, 1914), 2nd edn., I, par. 25. See Ernst Cassirer, *Kant's Life and Thought* (New Haven, 1981; 1st pub. 1918), pp. 327–9. A shift had occurred around midcentury in that earlier writers had considered sublimity

a quality inherent in things – in ideas, in objects, in words – while midcentury aestheticians and philosophers sought to locate sublimity in the process of perception; see Morris, *The Religious Sublime*, p. 180. Blair discussed both the sublimity inhering in objects and the sublimity of writing about such objects; *Lectures on Rhetoric*, p. 35.

55. Cassirer, *Kant*, p. 330.
56. Kant, *Critique of Judgment*, I, par. 23.
57. Cited by Guyer, *Kant*, p. 501.
58. Kant, *Critique of Judgment*, I, par. 26.
59. Hertz, *The End of the Line*, p. 40.
60. Kant, *Critique of Judgment*, I, par. 27.
61. Julie Ellison, "The Romantic Sublime and Romantic Irony," paper delivered at the Annual Meeting of the Modern Language Association, New York, 1983; my thanks to Professor Ellison for providing me with a copy of her paper. See also Thomas Weiskel, *The Romantic Sublime: Studies in the Structure and Psychology of Transcendence* (Baltimore and London, 1974), chs. 1 and 2.

3 The composition and reception of the "Jupiter" Symphony

1. Hildesheimer, *Mozart*; Braunbehrens, *Mozart in Vienna*; Steptoe, *Mozart–Da Ponte Operas*.
2. Deutsch, *Mozart Documents*, pp. 306–7.
3. Information in this paragraph assembled from Deutsch, *Mozart*; *Wolfgang Amadeus Mozart: Chronik eines Lebens*, comp. Joseph Heinz Eibl, 2nd edn. (Kassel, 1977); Mozart, *Verzeichnis aller meiner Werke*, ed. E. H. Mueller von Asow (Vienna, 1956); Steptoe, *Mozart–Da Ponte Operas*; Julia Moore, "Mozart in the Market-Place," *Journal of the Royal Musical Association* 114 (1989), 18–42; and the Köchel *Chronologisch-thematisches Verzeichnis sämtlicher Tonwerke Wolfgang Amadé Mozart*, 7th edn. (Wiesbaden, 1965).
4. Forkel, *Musikalischer Almanach 1789*, cited by Landon, *The Golden Years*, p. 192.
5. It was entered into his catalogue on 24 February; see Landon, *The Golden Years*, p. 192. Landon suggests that the work entered next, on 4 March, an aria he had already written for Aloysia Lange (née Weber), was perhaps performed by her as an entr'acte to the second oratorio evening.
6. Alan Tyson, *Mozart: Studies of the Autograph Scores* (Cambridge, Mass., 1987), p. 156.
7. The only other year with a relatively small number of works entered – 1784 with eleven – reflects both his large number of performing engagements, a sign of success, and a serious illness. 1785 saw twenty works, and 1786, nineteen. See also Steptoe, *Mozart–Da Ponte Operas*, p. 71, for a tabular distribution of "major works" in this period.
8. See Steptoe, *Mozart–Da Ponte Operas*, pp. 53–68. Julia Moore cites Johann Pezzl's *Skizze von Wien* (2nd edn. 1803) as suggesting that 550 gulden might maintain a modest bachelor for a year ("Mozart in the Market-Place," p. 28).
9. Anderson no. 554, pp. 915–16; *Mozart: Briefe und Aufzeichnungen*, ed. Wilhelm A. Bauer and Otto Erich Deutsch (Kassel, 1962), III, [Bauer-Deutsch] no. 1077.
10. Landon's hypotheses concerning these letters and dates of performance will be taken up in the next section.
11. Anderson no. 453, p. 808. Because of its celebratory function, the symphony originally had an opening march and second minuet, like a serenade.
12. Anderson no. 499, p. 859.
13. Deutsch, *Mozart*, p. 280, citing Hermann Abert, *W. A. Mozart*, 3 vols., 7th edn. (Leipzig, 1956). Because of the fragmentary nature of the sources, no record of any of these concerts is preserved. The work entered before the concerto is the B♭-major Piano Trio, K. 502, on 18 November.
14. Zaslaw, *Mozart Symphonies*, pp. 421–31.

15. Landon, *1791: Mozart's Last Year* (London and New York, 1988), pp. 31–5. Dexter Edge has collected preliminary evidence of other concert possibilities for Mozart's last three symphonies, which he plans to publish in the near future.
16. See Braunbehrens, *Mozart in Vienna*, pp. 284–90.
17. Anderson no. 545, pp. 905–6. The letter of November 1786 was no. 542, pp. 901–2.
18. Zaslaw, *Mozart's Symphonies*, p. 422.
19. Köchel, pp. 763–4 (K.Anh.A59). The leaf also contains an unidentified incipit.
20. Anderson no. 513, pp. 876–7.
21. On the other hand, as Zaslaw suggests, in the context of a discussion of Salzburg copyists, Mozart might well have meant *Michael* Haydn (*Mozart's Symphonies*, pp. 395–6).
22. See Sisman, *Haydn and the Classical Variation*, ch. 7.
23. As Jens Peter Larsen wrote, "It is natural to assume there was some connection"; "The Symphonies" in *The Mozart Companion*, ed. H. C. Robbins Landon and Donald Mitchell (London and New York, 1956), p. 184.
24. Tovey's article of 1929 on Brahms's chamber music, reprinted in *The Main Stream of Music and Other Essays* (Oxford, 1949; Cleveland and New York, 1959), contains this statement (pp. 259–60) about Brahms's Violoncello Sonata in F major, Op. 99, Violin Sonata in A major, Op. 100, and Piano Trio in C minor, Op. 101: "These three works were all produced in the same year, and (like Mozart's last three symphonies produced within six weeks) make an excellent concert programme, their contrasts being, in the nature of the case, exactly what represented the happiest reactions of the composer himself."
25. Stanley Sadie notes the "earlier pairings of works in G minor with others in E♭ (the piano quartets of 1785–6) and C major (the string quintets of 1787)"; see Sadie, *Mozart Symphonies* (London, 1986), p. 82.
26. See Rita Steblin, *History of Key Characteristics in the Eighteenth and Early Nineteenth Centuries* (Ann Arbor, 1983); her Appendix A presents summaries of theorists' views of each key.
27. Steblin, *Key Characteristics*, p. 245, quoting, respectively, Ribock (1783), Schubart (c. 1784), and R . . . r, G. G. in Cramer's *Magazin der Musik* (1786).
28. Ibid., p. 278, quoting, respectively, Schubart, Ribock, and Galeazzi (1796).
29. Ibid., p. 223, quoting, respectively, Schubart, R . . . r, G. G., and Galeazzi.
30. See H. C. Robbins Landon, *The Symphonies of Joseph Haydn* (London, 1955), *passim*; A. Peter Brown, "Eighteenth-Century Traditions and Mozart's Jupiter Symphony K. 551", paper presented at the Hofstra University Mozart Conference, February 1991.
31. Johann Pezzl, *Skizze von Wien* (Vienna, 1786–90), trans. in Landon, *Mozart and Vienna*, (London and New York, 1990), pp. 162–3.
32. Aleksandr Oulibicheff (Ulïbïchev), *Nouvelle Biographie de Mozart*, 3 vols. (Moscow, 1843), III, pp. 260–1; quoted from the excerpt trans. in A. Oulibicheff, "The 'Jupiter' Symphony of Mozart," *Dwight's Journal of Music* 27 (1867), 121–2. I use the spelling in *The New Grove*, XIX, p. 326.
33. Braunbehrens, *Mozart in Vienna*, p. 315.
34. Mozart, *Symphonie C (Jupiter)*, Philharmonia-Facsimiledrucke No. 2 (Vienna, 1923); Mozart, *Sinfonie in C*, ed. Karl-Heinz Köhler, Documenta Musicologica, Series 2, vol. 8 (Kassel, 1978). Köhler's introduction has more information on the history of the manuscript.
35. Information about the paper types and their arrangement in the autograph kindly supplied by Alan Tyson, who has been very generous to me with his Mozart materials.
36. A sampling of favorable early reviews of performances and editions between 1794 and 1828 appears at the end of Kunze's *Jupiter-Sinfonie*, pp. 129–33. A few unfavorable notices may be found in Georges de Saint-Foix, *The Symphonies of Mozart*, trans. Lesley Orrey (London, 1947; New York, 1968), pp. 177–8.
37. Ernst Ludwig Gerber, *Neues historisch-biographisches Lexikon der Tonkünstler* (Leipzig, 1812–14), ed. Othmar Wessely (Graz, 1966), III, col. 497.
38. Nissen, *Biographie*, Appendix, p. 157.

39. F . . . , "Bescheidene Anfrage an die modernsten Komponisten und Virtuosen," *Allgemeine musikalische Zeitung* 1 (1798), cols. 141–4, 152–5, at 153. Landon claims the piece is signed "Z . . ." and that the author must be Zelter (Landon, *Haydn Chronicle*, IV, p. 339); Zaslaw follows him in this (*Mozart's Symphonies*, p. 530). Landon translates the last phrase as "pushed things a little too far" (er's bekanntlich ein wenig arg macht).

40. Gernot Gruber, *Mozart und die Nachwelt* (Salzburg and Vienna, 1985), p. 155. Gruber's book is marred by scanty and imprecise documentation. See also Martin Staehelin, "Zum Verhältnis von Mozart- und Beethoven-Bild im 19. Jahrhundert," *Mozart-Jahrbuch 1980–3*, 17–22, and Herbert Schneider, "Probleme der Mozart-Rezeption im Frankreich der ersten Hälfte des 19. Jahrhunderts," *Mozart-Jahrbuch 1980–3*, 23–31.

41. Wolfgang Robert Griepenkerl, *Das Musikfest oder der Beethovener* (Braunschweig, 1838), quoted in Gruber, *Mozart und die Nachwelt*, p. 157.

42. R. Larry Todd, "Mozart according to Mendelssohn: A Contribution to *Rezeptionsgeschichte*," in *Perspectives on Mozart Performance*, ed. R. Larry Todd and Peter Williams (Cambridge, 1991), pp. 162–71; Richard Wagner, *Autobiographische Skizze* (1865), cited in Saint-Foix, *Symphonies of Mozart*, p. 178. Todd gives examples of Mendelssohn's compositions beside *Sinfonia VIII* that show the influence of the "Jupiter."

43. Todd, "Mozart according to Mendelssohn," p. 161. See the list of Mozart pieces and corresponding journal reviews and notices on pp. 176–82.

44. *Allgemeine musikalische Zeitung* 44 (1846), cols. 735–6.

45. *Allgemeine musikalische Zeitung* 7 (1805), col. 501, trans. in Mary Sue Morrow, "Of Unity and Passion: The Aesthetics of Concert Criticism in Early-Nineteenth-Century Vienna," *19th-Century Music* 13 (1990), 204.

46. Robert Schumann, *On Music and Musicians*, ed. Konrad Wolff, trans. Paul Rosenfeld (New York, 1946; Berkeley and Los Angeles, 1983), pp. 81–2. The context is an analysis of Hiller's studies for pianoforte.

47. Richard Heuberger, *Erinnerungen an Johannes Brahms*, ed. Kurt Hofmann (Tutzing, 1971), quoted by Imogen Fellinger, "Brahms's View of Mozart," in *Brahms: Biographical, Documentary and Analytical Studies*, ed. Robert Pascall (Cambridge, 1983), p. 55.

48. Gruber, *Mozart und die Nachwelt*, p. 218.

49. Oulibicheff (Ulïbichev), *Nouvelle Biographie de Mozart*, II, pp. 222–8 and III, pp. 260–6, quoted from trans. in *Dwight's Journal of Music* (see n. 32). The "Jupiter" was frequently performed in the Boston of that period; program notes to it were printed in the *Dwight's Journal of Music* of 9 November 1867, and a concert review on 23 November 1867 justified its reduced comments about the "Jupiter" by pointing out that it has been "too often heard and discussed here, to need any description."

50. I am indebted to Ian Bent for providing me with his translation of this work before publication of his volume on nineteenth-century analysis for Cambridge Readings in the Literature of Music. The original, "Zergliederung des Finale aus Mozarts 4tes Sinfonie in C," has been published in a modern edition as *Das Finale von W. A. Mozarts Jupiter-Symphonie*, ed. Friedrich Eckstein (Vienna, 1923).

51. These will be dealt with more fully in Chapter 8.

52. Saint-Foix, *Symphonies of Mozart*, pp. 145–8.

53. Sechter, "Zergliederung," trans. Ian Bent.

54. Johann Christian Lobe, *Lehrbuch der musikalischen Komposition*, III (Leipzig, 1860), pp. 393–431, at 393–4, 431.

55. Abert, *Mozart*. Saint-Foix describes the section on the late symphonies in Abert's book as "the most profound commentary to which the instrumental music of Mozart in its final stages has given rise" (*Symphonies of Mozart*, p. 154). Jahn's own commentary was rather general, seeking to characterize rather than to describe or analyze; see Jahn, *Life of Mozart*, III, pp. 37–9.

56. Abert, *Mozart*, II, p. 493.

57. Ibid., II, p. 498; Warren Kirkendale, *Fugue and Fugato in Rococo and Classical Chamber*

Music, 2nd rev. edn., trans. Margaret Bent and the author (Durham, N.C., 1979), pp. 91–2. Other examples are the slow movement of Quartet, K. 168, the fugue subject of Haydn's F-minor Quartet, Op. 20 No. 5, and "And with His Stripes" from Handel's *Messiah*.

58. Donald Francis Tovey, "Symphony in C Major (Köchel's Catalogue, No. 551)," *Essays in Musical Analysis: Symphonies and Other Works*, new edn. (Oxford, 1981), pp. 443–4.

59. Saint-Foix, *Symphonies of Mozart*, pp. 148–9. See n. 40.

60. Ibid., p. 177.

61. Alfred Einstein, *Mozart: His Character, His Work*, trans. Nathan Broder and Arthur Mendel (New York, 1945), ch. 9 ("Mozart and Counterpoint") and pp. 235–6. Specialized studies of Mozart's counterpoint include A. Hyatt King, "The Growth and Significance of Mozart's Counterpoint," in *Mozart in Retrospect*, pp. 164–79; Isabelle Emerson, "The Role of Counterpoint in the Formation of Mozart's Late Style" (Ph.D. diss., Columbia University, 1977); and Kirkendale, *Fugue and Fugato*, pp. 152–81.

62. See ch. 8, n. 7, where literature on this point is cited.

63. David, *Die Jupiter-Symphonie*, p. 9. Drawing on this book, William Klenz sought to show the entire ten-note formula as a "cryptogram" embedded in other Mozart works; see "*Per Aspera ad Astra* or The Stairway to Jupiter," *Music Review* 30 (1969), 169–210. Marius Flothuis suggests connections among the three last symphonies, on the one hand, and between these works and *Die Zauberflöte*, on the other; see "Jupiter oder Sarastro? Versuch über die wahre Art dreier Symphonien und einer Oper," *Mozart-Jahrbuch 1965/66*, 121–32.

64. King, *Mozart in Retrospect*, Appendix 2.

65. Ellwood Derr, "A Deeper Examination of Mozart's 1̂–2̂–4̂–3̂ Theme and Its Strategic Deployment," *In Theory Only* 8 (1985), 5–45.

66. Gerd Sievers, "Analyse des Finale aus Mozarts Jupiter-Symphonie," *Die Musikforschung* 7 (1954), 318–31; rpt. in *Zur musikalischen Analyse*, ed. Gerhard Schuhmacher, Wege der Forschung CCLVII (Darmstadt, 1974), pp. 72–95. See Chapter 8.

67. Susan Wollenberg, "The Jupiter Theme: New Light on Its Creation," *Musical Times* 116 (1975), 781–3. A. Peter Brown, in "Eighteenth-Century Traditions," has suggested that various *Alleluia* melodies are more convincing models, and he connects this with celebrating victories in the Turkish War, and with Mozart's *Alleluia* canon, K. 553, entered in his catalogue on 2 September 1788. Stanley Sadie has accepted the *Lucis creator* origin, and has included it in both *The New Grove Mozart* (New York, 1983) and *Mozart Symphonies*.

68. Katharine Thomson, *The Masonic Thread in Mozart* (London, 1977).

69. Ibid., pp. 129–30.

70. See ch. 1, n. 21.

71. *The Oxford Companion to Classical Literature*, ed. Paul Harvey, rev. edn. (Oxford, 1984), s.v. "Jupiter." This sentence does not appear in the new second edition, ed. M. C. Howatson. I am indebted to Michael Long for calling it to my attention.

72. Schroeder, *Haydn and the Enlightenment*, p. 118.

73. Of the studies published in the 1980s, I leave out of account the survey by Robert Dearling, *The Music of Wolfgang Amadeus Mozart: The Symphonies* (Rutherford, N.J., 1982) and the masterly BBC Music Guide by Stanley Sadie, *Mozart Symphonies*; the latter, within the size-limitation of its format, draws on the latest source research and has many fresh insights, beautifully expressed, about the music.

74. Zaslaw, *Mozart's Symphonies*, ch. 13, pp. 510–44.

75. Subotnik, "Evidence of a Critical World View in Mozart's Last Three Symphonies," in *Music and Civilization: Essays in Honor of Paul Henry Lang*, ed. Edmond Strainchamps and Maria Rika Maniates (New York, 1984), pp. 29–43; rpt. in Subotnik, *Developing Variations: Style and Ideology in Western Music* (Minneapolis, 1991), pp. 98–111. I find dubious here the thick overlay of jargon and ideology onto a study that remains coy about its methodology;

Subotnik's frequently reiterated notion of "concrete, cultural particularity" comes to seem a pair of concrete shoes for the "Jupiter."
76. Kunze, *Jupiter-Sinfonie*, pp. 119–28. See Chapter 8 of the present study.

4 Design: four movement-plans

1. Leo Treitler, "Mozart and the Idea of Absolute Music," in his *Music and the Historical Imagination* (Cambridge, Mass., 1989), p. 210. He goes on to say, apropos of Symphony No. 39/II, "But it is not."
2. See Sisman, *Haydn and the Classical Variation*, chs. 6–7.
3. See Zaslaw, *Mozart's Symphonies*, pp. 501–4; Hugh Macdonald, "To Repeat or Not to Repeat?," *Proceedings of the Royal Musical Association* 111 (1984–5), 121–8.
4. I prefer to save the term "transition" for local transitions between thematic groups, as in Symphony No. 40/I, bars 58–66.
5. For those readers who prefer the letters suggested by Jan LaRue – P, T, S, K – for primary, transitional (bridge), secondary, and closing functions, it ought to be an easy matter to make the mental substitutions. While they are useful, and widely used in the U.S., I simply find them less aesthetically pleasing.

5 Gesture and expectation: Allegro vivace

1. Respectively, Sadie, *Mozart Symphonies*, p. 128; Zaslaw, *Mozart's Symphonies*, p. 536; Ratner, *Classic Music*, p. 395.
2. Ratner, *Classic Music*; Allanbrook, *Rhythmic Gesture in Mozart*. V. Kofi Agawu, in *Playing with Signs: A Semiotic Interpretation of Classic Music* (Princeton, 1991), has applied Ratner's kind of topical analysis to a Schenkerian beginning–middle–end paradigm to arrive at a semiotic synthesis.
3. See Ratner, *Classic Music*; ch. 2; Agawu, *Playing with Signs*, p. 30; Allanbrook, *Rhythmic Gesture in Mozart*, part I.
4. The topical nature of learned style will be examined in Chapter 8. Agawu's *Playing with Signs* critiques the notion of topical limits.
5. See Ratner, *Classic Music*, p. 103.
6. Letter of 12 June 1778; Anderson no. 309a, p. 553.
7. Alan Tyson has suggested that the Finale of the "Prague" symphony was composed first, because Mozart intended it as the new Finale to K. 297; see Tyson, *Mozart*, pp. 21–2. Possibly this explains the *coups d'archet* in the "Prague" introduction.
8. These figures are discussed by Forkel, *Allgemeine Geschichte*, pp. 53–9, with examples from C. P. E. Bach.
9. See Vickers, *In Defence of Rhetoric*, pp. 284, 492.
10. Charles Rosen, *The Classical Style* (New York, 1971), p. 335.
11. Rosen discusses the very common move to V/vi as a way of avoiding a cadence on vi to end the development; *Sonata Forms*, rev. edn. (New York, 1988), pp. 267–72. The submediant was the most common key-goal for the development.
12. Oliver Strunk, "Haydn's Divertimenti for Baryton, Viola, and Bass," *Musical Quarterly* 18 (1932), 236; Bonds, "Haydn's False Recapitulations," pp. 220–4. Bonds gives a valuable summary of various kinds of recapitulations, pp. 207–33.
13. Rosen, *Sonata Forms*, p. 282.
14. James Webster, "Sonata Form," in *The New Grove*, XVII, p. 502.
15. Janet M. Levy, "Texture as a Sign in Classic and Early Romantic Music," *Journal of the American Musicological Society* 35 (1982), 483.
16. Rosen, *Sonata Forms*, p. 280; he is, however, describing an actual false recapitulation.

17. Levy, "Texture as a Sign," p. 497. See also Beth Shamgar, "On Locating the Retransition in Classic Sonata Form," *Music Review* 42 (1981), 130–43.
18. A. Peter Brown likened this passage to the duel in the first scene of *Don Giovanni*, in "Eighteenth-Century Traditions."
19. Jane R. Stevens, "Georg Joseph Vogler and the 'Second Theme' in Sonata Form," *Journal of Musicology* 2 (1983), 278–304.
20. Koch, *Versuch*, III, trans. Nancy K. Baker as *Introductory Essay on Composition*, p. 199.
21. See Sisman, *Haydn and the Classical Variation*, ch. 4.

6 Structure and expression: Andante cantabile

1. The lengths of the slow movements of the late symphonies are: No. 38, 148 bars; No. 39, 161 bars; No. 40, 123 bars; No. 41, 101 bars. The "Jupiter" thus returns in length to the "Linz," 104 bars. The "Haffner" was only 84 bars.
2. On the orchestration in Mozart's concertos, with a few examples from the "Prague," see Irving R. Eisley, "Mozart's Concertato Orchestra," *Mozart-Jahrbuch 1976/7*, 9–20.
3. Leo Treitler, "Mozart and the Idea of Absolute Music," pp. 176–214.
4. Ibid., pp. 206–7.
5. Other musicologists must also surely have remarked that the E♭-major Andante of Haydn's G-minor Symphony No. 83, "La Poule," has an ascending repeated-note main theme with imitation in the bass, subsequently repeated with a countermelody, that resembles Mozart's No. 40.
6. Letter to his father of 9 June 1784; Anderson no. 515, p. 880.
7. The possibility of operatic echoes in these symphonies ought not to be discounted. Certainly the incandescent pastoral world of the "Prague's" Andante resembles that of *Figaro*, while the slow introduction to the "Prague" proleptically suggests both *Don Giovanni* and, in bars 16–19, the Queen of the Night. (The "Papageno-world" of the finale of the G-major piano concerto, K. 453, has been often suggested.)
8. The D♭-major passage in the exposition of No. 40 (G♭ in the recapitulation) is just such a progression. And while the stable passage in the dominant in No. 39 does not follow the harmonic pattern, its suspensions cast it in this mold as well.
9. For an elegant voice-leading analysis of K. 453/II, see Carl Schachter, "Idiosyncratic Features of Three Mozart Slow Movements, K. 449, K. 453, and K. 467," in *Mozart's Piano Concertos: Text, Context, Interpretation*, ed. Neal Zaslaw (Ann Arbor, [1993]).
10. Ratner, *Classic Music*, pp. 11–12. Allanbrook also discusses the sarabande as a topic in *Rhythmic Gesture in Mozart*, pp. 37–8; of the "Dissonant" she writes, "In moments where the dotted pattern is not evident, Mozart still retains the emphasis on the second beat in a free and elegant play on the sarabande pattern."
11. On the terms "slow-movement sonata form" and "secondary development," see Charles Rosen, *Sonata Forms* (New York, 1980; 1988), pp. 106–12. He gives a lengthy example of the secondary development in the "Dissonant" slow movement.
12. Susan McClary gives this movement an overheated ideological reading in "A Musical Dialectic from the Enlightenment: Mozart's *Piano Concerto in G Major, K. 453*, Movement 2," *Cultural Critique* 4 (1986), 129–69, in which she interprets the soloist's outbursts as the cry of the individual against the oppressive State-sponsored Enlightenment rationality. For her the saddest moment occurs when the soloist returns to the tonic: "the social norm comes to the fore and stamps out the deviant strain. It might be argued that the orchestra does so for the soloist's own good – that is, rescues and returns it to the safety and security of the tonic key area – but that is the kind of argument that leads to politically motivated psychiatric treatment. If eighteenth-century musical procedures purport to be based on the premise that harmony between social order and individual freedom is possible, then this version of the moment shows

the authoritarian force that social convention will draw upon if confronted by recalcitrant nonconformity" (p. 151).

13. These C-major bars are remarkably close to C. P. E. Bach's Hamburg Symphony in C major, W. 182 No. 3 (1772). And a lyrical theme undone by bass figuration was to reemerge dramatically in the "Scene in the country" movement of Berlioz's *Symphonie fantastique*.

7 Phrase rhythm: Menuetto, Allegretto

1. Georg August Griesinger, *Biographische Notizen über Joseph Haydn* (Leipzig, 1810), trans. Gotwals as *Haydn: Two Contemporary Portraits*, p. 61.
2. Leonard B. Meyer, "Grammatical Simplicity and Relational Richness: The Trio of Mozart's G Minor Symphony," *Critical Inquiry* 2 (1976), 693–761.
3. Ibid., 693–4; his earlier assertion appeared in *Music, the Arts, and Ideas* (Chicago, 1967), ch. 2, "Some Remarks on Value and Greatness in Music."
4. Meyer, "Grammatical Simplicity," p. 698.
5. Interestingly, the only minuets by Mozart that begin quietly with a blurred downbeat are in the C-major chamber music for strings, Quartet, K. 465 and Quintet, K. 515.
6. Meredith Ellis Little, "Minuet" in *The New Grove*, XII, p. 354.
7. Zaslaw points out that this movement has Mozart's only separate cello and bass parts in the symphonies; *Mozart's Symphonies*, p. 537.
8. Koch, *Introductory Essay*, pp. 1–40.
9. Ratner, *Classic Music*, p. 39. Thomas Clifton also comments briefly on this piece as a form of witticism involving temporal reversal, in *Music as Heard: A Study in Applied Phenomenology* (New Haven, 1983), p. 268. Jonathan Kramer analyzes it in more detail in *The Time of Music* (New York, 1988), pp. 144–8.
10. Arthur Quinn, *Figures of Speech* (Salt Lake City, 1982), p. 43. He gives an example from Virgil: "Let us die, and rush into the heart of the fight."
11. The Menuetto of the "Dissonant" String Quartet, K. 465, also in C major, actually begins with the same kind of eighth-note writing that characterizes the true "beginning" in K. 551, bar 3. The only full-bar chord in the Quartet minuet is the deliberate action-stopping V_5^6/V in bar 12.

8 The rhetoric of the learned style: Finale, Molto allegro

1. Einstein, *Mozart*, p. 235. The Michael Haydn Symphony, P. 31, has an autograph dated 19 February 1788, and is published in *M. Haydn: Instrumentalwerke*, ed. L. Perger, Denkmäler der Tonkunst in Österreich, XXIV, Jg. 14/2.
2. Leopold Mozart, *Versuch einer gründlichen Violinschule* (Augsburg, 1756); trans. Editha Knocker as *A Treatise on the Fundamental Principles of Violin Playing* (Oxford, 1945; 1988), p. 166. Quintilian had commented that metaphor is "so natural a turn of speech that it is often employed unconsciously or by uneducated persons," and that hyperbole "is employed even by peasants and uneducated persons, for the good reason that everybody has an innate passion for exaggeration." Quintilian, *Institutio oratoria*, VIII. vi. 4 and VIII. vi. 75 respectively, cited by Vickers, *In Defence of Rhetoric*, p. 299.
3. Another portion of Mozart's letter (Anderson no. 833) is cited in Chapter 2, p. 15; Quintilian, *Institutio oratoria*, VIII. ii. 22, p. 209; Aristotle, *"Art" of Rhetoric*, trans. John Henry Freese, Loeb Classical Library (Cambridge, Mass., 1926), III. xii. 6, p. 425.
4. Johann Georg Albrechtsberger, *Collected Writings on Thorough-Bass, Harmony, and Counterpoint for Self-Instruction*, ed. Ignaz von Seyfried, trans. Sabilla Novello, 2nd edn. (London, 1855), p. 197.
5. Ratner, *Classic Music*, p. 23.

6. Giorgio Pestelli, *The Age of Mozart and Beethoven*, trans. Eric Cross (Cambridge, 1984), pp. 136–7.

7. Distinctions of this kind were made by Marpurg, Quantz, C. P. E. Bach, Kirnberger, Scheibe, Türk, and Koch. For references, see David A. Sheldon, "The Galant Style Revisited and Re-evaluated," *Acta Musicologica* (1975), 261–2, and "The Concept *Galant* in the 18th Century," *Journal of Musicological Research* 9 (1989), 89–108.

8. Albrechtsberger, *Anweisung zur Composition* (Vienna, 1790), p. 172, quoted in Kirkendale, *Fugue and Fugato*, p. 76.

9. Motivic imitation may include canonic techniques as in the first movement development section of the "Prague."

10. Karl Schrauf, "Des P. Gratian Marx ursprünglicher Entwurf für die Reform der österreichischen Gymnasium vom 7. Juli 1775," *Mitteilungen der Gesellschaft für deutsche Erziehungs- und Schulgeschichte* 6 (1896), 37, cited in Georg Jäger, "Zur literarischen Gymnasialbildung in Österreich von der Aufklärung bis zum Vormärz," in *Die Österreichische Literatur*, p. 92.

11. Albrechtsberger, *Collected Writings*, pp. 197, 219.

12. Forkel, *Allgemeine Geschichte der Musik*, I, pp. 47–8.

13. Ibid, p. 48. He also broadened "fugue" to include "polyphonische Compositionsart" in a footnote on p. 48. For a view of fugue as part of eighteenth-century intellectual development, see David Sheldon, "The Fugue as an Expression of Rationalist Values," *International Review of the Aesthetics and Sociology of Music* 17 (1986), 29–51.

14. Quintilian, *Institutio oratoria*, IX. i. 10, 11, 13. Rhetorical figures, termed "aids to expression" by Forkel (*Allgemeine Geschichte der Musik*, I, p. 53), were also variously identified and classified in the eighteenth century, especially by Mattheson, Scheibe, and Forkel himself, following the tradition inaugurated by Burmeister's *Musica poetica* in 1606.

15. Forkel differentiated between "figures for the intellect (*Verstand*)," which included contrapuntal devices and textures, and "figures for the imagination (*Einbildungskraft*)," comprising musical "painting" and "imitations" of externally visible and aural phenomena (*Gegenstände*) and, more profoundly, of internal feelings; Forkel, *Allgemeine Geschichte der Musik*, I, pp. 54–5. It seems clear that these categories can intersect.

16. Sheldon, "The Concept *Galant*," and literature cited there; Carl Dahlhaus, "The Eighteenth-Century as a Music-Historical Epoch," trans. Ernest Harriss, *College Music Symposium* 26 (1986), 1–6.

17. This abstract is given in James J. Murphy, *Rhetoric in the Middle Ages* (Berkeley and Los Angeles, 1974), p. 179.

18. Translation altered from Anderson, no. 476, according to the original in *Mozart: Briefe und Aufzeichnungen*, ed. Wilhelm A. Bauer and Otto Erich Deutsch (Kassel, 1962), III, no. 715.

19. The recapitulation begins with the bridge passage in the subdominant, then offers just the double fugue from the second group before the closing section.

20. The only exception that I have found is Haydn's Symphony No. 70 in D major (*c*. 1779), which has an introduction based on the fugue subject. I leave out of account rondos and variations with fugal episodes, such as the finales of the F-major Piano Concerto, K. 459, and Haydn's "Clock" Symphony, No. 101.

21. This sort of "doubleness" is actually present in other ways throughout the movement; for example, even in 1a, the bass line is a kind of stretto inversion of the four-note motive.

22. Cicero, *De inventione*, trans. H. M. Hubbell, Loeb Classical Library (Cambridge, Mass., 1949), I. xv. 20, p. 43.

23. See Warren Kirkendale, "Ciceronians versus Aristotelians on the Ricercar as Exordium, from Bembo to Bach," *Journal of the American Musicological Society* 32 (1979), 26–7. Zaslaw plausibly interprets the subject as "Mozart's creed," because of Mozart's earlier use of it in his Missa

brevis in F major (K. 192/186f); see *Mozart's Symphonies*, p. 537, as well as pp. 537–44 for more controversial hypotheses outlined in Chapter 3, pp. 35–6

24. Cited from the *Berlinische musikalische Zeitung* 1 (1805), 179, and trans. in Peter le Huray and James Day, *Music and Aesthetics in the Eighteenth and Early-Nineteenth Centuries* (Cambridge, 1981), p. 290. Many other writers on the sublime, including Sulzer, Crotch, Schilling, and Lichtenthal, are excerpted in this volume.

25. See Edward T. Cone, "On Derivation: Syntax and Rhetoric," *Music Analysis* 6 (1987), 246.

26. Enriched by the themes of a sonata-form design, it makes the earlier purely learned fugue (1B) pallid by contrast.

27. The image is made explicit by Sulzer, "Erhaben," in *Allgemeine Theorie*, II, p. 98, and Morris, *Religious Sublime* (see Chapter 2, n. 21).

Select bibliography

Abert, Hermann, *W. A. Mozart*, 7th edn. (Leipzig, 1956)

Agawu, V. Kofi, *Playing with Signs: A Semiotic Interpretation of Classic Music* (Princeton, 1991)

Allanbrook, Wye J., *Rhythmic Gesture in Mozart: Le nozze di Figaro and Don Giovanni* (Chicago, 1983)

Anderson, Emily (trans. and ed.), *The Letters of Mozart and His Family*, 3rd edn. (New York, 1985)

Autexier, Philippe A., "La Musique Maçonnique," *Dix-Huitième Siècle* 19 (1987), 97–104

Biba, Otto, "Grundzüge des Konzertwesens in Wien zu Mozarts Zeit," *Mozart-Jahrbuch 1978/9*, 132–43

Bonds, Mark Evan, *Wordless Rhetoric: Musical Form and the Metaphor of the Oration* (Cambridge, Mass., 1991)

Braunbehrens, Volkmar, *Mozart in Vienna, 1781–1791*, trans. Timothy Bell (New York, 1989)

Brion, Marcel, *Daily Life in the Vienna of Mozart and Schubert*, trans. Jean Stewart (New York, 1962)

Broyles, Michael, "The Two Instrumental Styles of Classicism," *Journal of the American Musicological Society* 36 (1983), 210–42

Burney, Charles, *An Eighteenth-Century Musical Tour in Central Europe and the Netherlands. Dr. Burney's Musical Tours in Europe*, ed. Percy A. Scholes, II (London, 1959)

Churgin, Bathia, "The Symphony as Described by J. A. P. Schulz: A Commentary and Translation," *Current Musicology* 29 (1980), 7–16

David, Johann Nepomuk, *Die Jupiter-Symphonie: Eine Studie über die thematisch-melodischen Zusammenhänge* (Göttingen, 1953)

Dearling, Robert, *The Music of Wolfgang Amadeus Mozart: The Symphonies* (Rutherford, N.J., 1982)

Derr, Ellwood, "A Deeper Examination of Mozart's $\hat{1}$–$\hat{2}$–$\hat{4}$–$\hat{3}$ Theme and Its Strategic Deployment," *In Theory Only* 8 (1985), 5–45

Deutsch, Otto Erich, *Mozart: A Documentary Biography* (London and Stanford, 1965)

Edge, Dexter, Review Article of Mary Sue Morrow, *Concert Life in Haydn's Vienna*, *Haydn Yearbook* 17 (1992), 108–66

Einstein, Alfred, *Mozart: His Character, His Work*, trans. Nathan Broder and Arthur Mendel (New York, 1945)

Eisley, Irving R., "Mozart's Concertato Orchestra," *Mozart-Jahrbuch 1976/7*, 9–20

Flothuis, Marius, "Jupiter oder Sarastro? Versuch über die wahre Art dreier Symphonien und einer Oper," *Mozart-Jahrbuch* 1965/6, 121–32

Forkel, Johann Nikolaus, *Allgemeine Geschichte der Musik* (Leipzig, 1788–1801)

Gruber, Gernot, *Mozart und die Nachwelt* (Salzburg and Vienna, 1983)

"Johann August Apel und eine Diskussion um Ästhetik der Sinfonie im frühen 19. Jahrhundert," in *Studien zur Instrumentalmusik: Lothar Hoffmann-Erbrecht zum 60. Geburtstag*, ed. Anke Bingmann, Klaus Hortschansky, and Winfried Kirsch (Tutzing, 1988), pp. 261–83

Harrison, Daniel, "Rhetoric and Fugue: An Analytical Application," *Music Theory Spectrum* 12 (1990), 1–42

Heartz, Daniel, "Thomas Attwood's Lessons in Composition with Mozart," *Proceedings of the Royal Musical Association* 100 (1973–4), 175–83

Hertz, Neil, *The End of the Line: Essays on Psychoanalysis and the Sublime* (New York, 1985)

Hildesheimer, Wolfgang, *Mozart*, trans. Marion Faber (New York, 1982)

Kennedy, George A., *Classical Rhetoric and Its Christian and Secular Tradition from Ancient to Modern Times* (Chapel Hill, 1980)

King, A. Hyatt, *Mozart in Retrospect: Studies in Criticism and Bibliography* (Oxford, 1955; 3rd rev. edn., 1970)

Kirkendale, Warren, *Fugue and Fugato in Rococo and Classical Chamber Music*, trans. Margaret Bent and the author, 2nd edn. (Durham, N.C., 1979)

Kunze, Stefan, *Wolfgang Amadeus Mozart: Sinfonie in C-Dur KV 551, Jupiter-Sinfonie* (Munich, 1988)

Landon, H. C. Robbins, *Mozart: The Golden Years, 1781–1791* (London and New York, 1989)

1791: Mozart's Last Year (London and New York, 1988)

Mozart and Vienna (London and New York, 1990)

le Huray, Peter and Day, James, *Music and Aesthetics in the Eighteenth and Early-Nineteenth Centuries* (Cambridge, 1981)

Levy, Janet M., "Texture as a Sign in Classic and Early Romantic Music," *Journal of the American Musicological Society* 35 (1982), pp. 482–531

Lobe, Johann Christian, *Lehrbuch der musikalischen Komposition*, III (Leipzig, 1860), pp. 393–431

Meyer, Leonard, "Grammatical Simplicity and Relational Richness: The Trio of Mozart's G Minor Symphony," *Critical Inquiry* 2 (1976), 693–761

Monk, Samuel, *The Sublime: A Study of Critical Theories in XVIII-Century England* (1935; Ann Arbor, 1960)

Moore, Julia, "Mozart in the Market-Place," *Journal of the Royal Musical Association* 114 (1989), 18–42

Morrow, Mary Sue, *Concert Life in Haydn's Vienna: Aspects of a Developing Musical and Social Institution* (New York, 1989)

"Of Unity and Passion: The Aesthetics of Concert Criticism in Early Nineteenth-Century Vienna," *19th-Century Music* 13 (1990), 193–206

Niemetschek, Franz Xaver, *Leben des K. K. Kapellmeisters Wolfgang Gottlieb Mozart* (Prague, 1798), ed. Jost Perfahl as *Ich kannte Mozart* (Munich, 1984)

Nissen, Georg Nikolaus von, *Biographie W. A. Mozarts* (1828; Hildesheim, 1984)

Novello, Vincent and Mary, *A Mozart Pilgrimage. Being the Travel Diaries of Vincent and Mary Novello in the Year 1829*, transcribed and compiled by Nerina Medici di Marignano, ed. Rosemary Hughes (London, 1955)

Pestelli, Giorgio, *The Age of Mozart and Beethoven*, trans. Eric Cross (Cambridge, 1984)

Ratner, Leonard, *Classic Music: Expression, Form, and Style* (New York, 1980)

Rosen, Charles, *The Classical Style: Haydn, Mozart, Beethoven* (New York, 1971; London and Boston, 1976)

Sonata Forms (New York, 1980, 1988)

Sadie, Stanley, *Mozart Symphonies* (London, 1986)

The New Grove Mozart (London and New York, 1983)

Saint-Foix, Georges de, *The Symphonies of Mozart*, trans. Lesley Orrey (London, 1947; New York, 1968)

Schroeder, David P., *Haydn and the Enlightenment* (Oxford, 1990)

Sechter, Simon, *Das Finale von W. A. Mozarts Jupiter-Symphonie* (1843), ed. Friedrich Eckstein (Vienna, 1923)

Shamgar, Beth, "On Locating the Retransition in Classic Sonata Form," *Music Review* 42 (1981), 130–43

Sheldon, David, "The Galant Style Revisited and Re-evaluated," *Acta Musicologica* 47 (1975), 240–70

"The Concept Galant in the 18th Century," *Journal of Musicological Research* 9 (1989), 89–108

"The Fugue as an Expression of Rationalist Values," *International Review of the Aesthetics and Sociology of Music* 17 (1986), 29–51

Sievers, Gerd, "Analyse des Finale aus Mozarts Jupiter-Symphonie," *Die Musikforschung* 7 (1954), 318–31; rpt. in *Zur musikalischen Analyse*, ed. Gerhard Schuhmacher, Wege der Forschung (Darmstadt, 1974) CCLVII, pp. 72–95

Sisman, Elaine R., "Haydn's Theater Symphonies," *Journal of the American Musicological Society* 43 (1990), 292–352

Haydn and the Classical Variation (Cambridge, Mass., and London, 1993)

Steblin, Rita, *History of Key Characteristics in the Eighteenth and Early Nineteenth Centuries* (Ann Arbor, 1983)

Steptoe, Andrew, *The Mozart–Da Ponte Operas: The Cultural and Musical Background to Le nozze di Figaro, Don Giovanni, and Così fan tutte* (Oxford, 1988)

Subotnik, Rose Rosengard, "Evidence of a Critical World View in Mozart's Last Three Symphonies," in *Music and Civilization: Essays in Honor of Paul Henry Lang*, ed. Edmond Strainchamps and Maria Rika Maniates (New York, 1984), pp. 29–43; rpt. in Subotnik, *Developing Variations: Style and Ideology in Western Music* (Minneapolis, 1991), pp. 98–111

Thomson, Katharine, *The Masonic Thread in Mozart* (London, 1977)

Todd, R. Larry and Peter Williams (eds.), *Perspectives on Mozart Performance* (Cambridge, 1991)

Treitler, Leo, *Music and the Historical Imagination* (Cambridge, Mass., 1989)

Tyson, Alan, *Mozart: Studies of the Autograph Scores* (Cambridge, Mass., 1987)

Ulïbïchev (Oulibicheff), A., *Nouvelle Biographie de Mozart* (Moscow, 1843), p. 105

Vickers, Brian, *In Defence of Rhetoric* (Oxford, 1988)

Webster, James, *Haydn's "Farewell" Symphony and the Idea of Classical Style: Through-Composition and Cyclic Integration in His Instrumental Music* (Cambridge, 1991)

Wollenberg, Susan, "The Jupiter Theme: New Light on Its Creation," *Musical Times* 116 (1975), 781–3

Zaslaw, Neal, *Mozart's Symphonies: Context, Performance Practice, Reception* (Oxford, 1989)

Index

Abert, Hermann, 32–3
Albrechtsberger, Johann Georg, 69, 70
Allanbrook, Wye J., 46
Aristotle, 10, 69
Attwood, Thomas, 24–5
Augarten, 2, 4
Autexier, Philippe A., 35

Bach, Carl Philipp Emanuel, 21,
    99 n. 13, 100 n. 7
Bach, Johann Christian, 7
Bach, Johann Sebastian, 31, 82, 83
Beautiful, the, 16–17, 18–19, 20, 91 n. 33
Beethoven, Ludwig van, 29, 30; First
    Symphony, 30, 49; Second Sym-
    phony, 30; *Eroica* Symphony, 30;
    Fifth Symphony, x, 33; Ninth
    Symphony, x
Berlioz, Hector, 31, *Symphonie
    fantastique*, 99 n. 13
Binary (two-reprise) form, 8, 38, 63
Blair, Hugh, 15, 17
Boileau, Nicolas, 14
Bonds, Mark Evan, 51
Brahms, Johannes, 30
Braunbehrens, Volkmar, 21, 27
Broyles, Michael, 2
Buelow, George J., 11
Burgtheater, 1, 2, 4, 21
Burke, Edmund, 16–17, 18, 19, 20
Burney, Charles, 5, 16

Canon, x, 32, 39, 79; *see also* Mozart,
    "Jupiter" Symphony, canon in
Cantus firmus, 34
Cicero, 10, 75
Circle of fifths progression, 42, 44, 55
Compositional process, 30
Concerts: programs, 1, 6–7; types, 4;
venues, 1–4; see also Mozart, and
    concerts
Concerts de la Loge Olympique, 4
Cone, Edward, 78
Corelli, Arcangelo, 58
Counterpoint, 3, 10, 30, 32, 33, 34, 35,
    36, 39, 49, 69–71, 75–7, 79, 81,
    82–3

Daube, Johann Friedrich, 53
David, Johann Nepomuk, 34
Demetrius, 89 n. 6
Denis, Michael, 15–16, 72
Derr, Ellwood, 34
Dies, Albert Christoph, 6
Dittersdorf, Karl Ditters von, 4, 7;
    Symphonies on Ovid's *Metamor-
    phoses*, 4
D'Ogny, Comte, 4

Eberl, Anton, 30
Einstein, Albert, 34, 68, 71
Esterházy, Count Johann, 3, 5
Esterházy, Prince Nikolaus, 4
Eybler, Joseph Leopold, 7

False recapitulations, 50–3
Fischer, Johann Christian, 7
Forkel, Johann Nikolaus, 10, 11, 70
Freemasonry, 13, 35; lodges and con-
    certs, 5; and rhetoric, 13
Fugue, fugato, 1, 10, 31, 35, 36, 68, 69–
    72, 74, 75, 83; "pathotype" sub-
    ject, 33; "galantry" fugue, 69; *see
    also* Mozart, "Jupiter" Symphony,
    fugue in
Fux, Johann Joseph, 34

Galitzin (Golitzin), Prince, 3

106

Also of interest

Bach: Mass in B Minor

John Butt
University of California at Berkeley

The Mass in B Minor is arguably Bach's greatest single work. This guide considers the work from many angles, offering the reader basic information in a concise and accessible form. John Butt gives an absorbing account of the work's genesis, its historical context, and its reception by later generations. He considers the Mass, movement by movement, providing the text in both Latin and English, and suggests some new approaches to the work – its forms, style and overall structure. This is an informative and lucid guide, providing an up-to-date summary of existing research and opinions together with some new and challenging insights.

Berg: Violin Concerto

Anthony Pople
University of Lancaster

Described by Aaron Copland as 'among the finest creations of the modern repertoire', Berg's Violin Concerto has become a twentieth-century classic. In this authoritative and highly readable guide, the reader is introduced not only to the concerto itself but to all that surrounded and determined its composition.

The book puts the concerto in its cultural context, provides biographical information on the composers and others associated with the work, gives an accessible guide to the music and provides scholarly discussion for specialists. The author's ability to combine musical anecdote with scholarly analysis makes this guide compelling reading for amateur and specialist alike.

Beethoven: Missa solemnis

William Drabkin
University of Southampton

The *Missa solemnis* is a document of extraordinary richness from the last decades of Beethoven's creative life. In this compendious and accessible guide, William Drabkin considers the work as an expression of the most celebrated text of the Roman Catholic faith and as an example from a tradition of Mass settings in eighteenth- and early nineteenth-century Austria. The opening chapters present various critical perspectives on the *Missa solemnis* and chart the history of its composition, first performances and publication. But, above all, the work itself is considered in detail, including the overall design, connections between the movements, the orchestration, word painting and programmatic elements.

Chopin: The Four Ballades

Jim Samson
University of Exeter

Chopin's four ballades are widely regarded as being amongst the most significant extended works for solo piano of the nineteenth century. In an illuminating discussion, Jim Samson combines history and analysis to provide a comprehensive picture of these popular piano works, investigating the social and musical background to Chopin's unique style. He also evaluates the many printed editions of the ballades before considering their critical reception and the differing interpretations of well-known nineteenth- and twentieth-century pianists.

Mahler: Symphony No. 3

Peter Franklin

Lecturer in Music,
University of Leeds

Mahler's Third Symphony was conceived as a musical picture of the natural world. This handbook describes the composition of Mahler's grandiose piece of philosophical programme music in the context of the ideas that inspired it and the artistic debates and social conflicts that it reflects. In this original and wide-ranging account, Peter Franklin takes the Third Symphony as a representative modern European symphony of its period and evaluates the piece as both the culmination of Mahler's early symphonic style and a work whose contradictory effects mirror the complexity of contemporary social and musical manners. The music is described in detail, movement by movement, with chapters on the genesis, early performance and subsequent reception of the work.

Haydn: String Quartets, Op. 50

W. Dean Sutcliffe

St Catharine's College, Cambridge

The Op. 50 string quartets contain some of the purest writing Haydn ever accomplished. This first full account of the six quartets evaluates the Op. 50 in relation to Haydn's more frequently performed quartets and considers their relevance to Haydn's wider output.

The background to these works includes a brief history of the string quartet and an assessment of Haydn's earlier works in this genre and of his role at Esterháza. The description of the composition and publication of the Op. 50 quartets is based on the evidence of Haydn's surviving letters and the recently discovered autograph copies of numbers 3 to 6 – a discovery which is vividly documented here for the first time.